50 Premium Coffee Recipes for Home

By: Kelly Johnson

Table of Contents

- Classic Espresso
- Cappuccino
- Latte
- Macchiato
- Americano
- Flat White
- Mocha
- Cortado
- Affogato
- Cold Brew Coffee
- Nitro Coffee
- Irish Coffee
- Vietnamese Coffee
- Turkish Coffee
- Espresso Martini
- Coffee Tiramisu
- Coffee Crème Brûlée
- Coffee Gelato
- Coffee Cheesecake
- Coffee Caramel Sauce
- Coffee Brownies
- Coffee Macarons
- Coffee Granita
- Coffee Panna Cotta
- Coffee Truffles
- Coffee Banana Bread
- Coffee Almond Cake
- Coffee Ice Cream Sundae
- Coffee Scones
- Coffee Muffins
- Coffee Shortbread Cookies
- Coffee Chocolate Bark
- Coffee Cupcakes
- Coffee Creme Fraiche Dip
- Coffee-Rubbed Steak
- Coffee Chili

- Coffee-Infused Barbecue Sauce
- Coffee-Soaked Beef Brisket
- Coffee-Glazed Chicken Wings
- Coffee Marinade for Pork
- Coffee-Flavored Whipped Cream
- Coffee Syrup
- Coffee Pancakes
- Coffee French Toast
- Coffee Smoothie
- Coffee Milkshake
- Coffee Infused Hot Chocolate
- Coffee Poached Pears
- Coffee and Nut Clusters
- Coffee Custard

Classic Espresso

Ingredients:

- Freshly ground espresso coffee beans
- Water (filtered or bottled)

Equipment:

- Espresso machine or stovetop espresso maker (Moka pot)
- Coffee grinder (if using whole beans)

Instructions:

1. **Preheat the Machine:**
    - If you're using an espresso machine, turn it on and let it fully heat up. If using a Moka pot, fill the bottom chamber with water and place it on the stove to preheat.
2. **Grind the Coffee Beans:**
    - For best results, grind your coffee beans to a fine consistency just before brewing. You'll need about 1 to 2 tablespoons (7-14 grams) of coffee grounds per shot of espresso.
3. **Prepare the Portafilter:**
    - If using an espresso machine, place the ground coffee into the portafilter and tamp it down evenly with a tamper to ensure a uniform extraction.
4. **Brew the Espresso:**
    - **Espresso Machine:** Lock the portafilter into the machine and start the brew cycle. Aim for a brewing time of about 25-30 seconds to extract a rich, dark shot of espresso.
    - **Moka Pot:** Assemble the Moka pot, place it on medium heat, and wait until the coffee starts to sputter out of the spout. Once the sputtering slows, remove the pot from the heat.
5. **Serve Immediately:**
    - Serve the espresso immediately in a pre-warmed cup. Enjoy as is, or with a touch of sugar or milk if preferred.

Tips:

- **Coffee Freshness:** Use freshly roasted and ground coffee beans for the best flavor.
- **Tamping Pressure:** Apply consistent and firm pressure when tamping the grounds to ensure even extraction.
- **Temperature:** Ensure your water is at the right temperature (around 190-200°F or 90-95°C) for optimal extraction.

Enjoy your perfectly brewed Classic Espresso!

Cappuccino

Ingredients:

- 1 shot (1 ounce) of freshly brewed espresso
- 4 ounces of milk
- Cocoa powder or cinnamon (optional, for garnish)

Equipment:

- Espresso machine with a steam wand or a milk frother
- Coffee grinder (if using whole beans)

Instructions:

1. **Prepare the Espresso:**
   - Brew 1 shot (1 ounce) of espresso using an espresso machine or a stovetop espresso maker. Pour it into a pre-warmed cappuccino cup.
2. **Steam the Milk:**
   - **With an Espresso Machine:** Fill the milk pitcher with 4 ounces of cold milk. Insert the steam wand into the pitcher and turn on the steam. Position the wand just below the surface of the milk and steam until the milk is frothy and reaches about 150-160°F (65-70°C). Aim for a creamy, velvety texture with a good amount of foam.
   - **With a Milk Frother:** If using a standalone milk frother, heat the milk according to the manufacturer's instructions and froth it until it has a rich foam.
3. **Combine the Espresso and Milk:**
   - Gently swirl the milk to combine the froth with the liquid. Pour the steamed milk over the espresso, holding back the foam with a spoon to layer it on top. The foam should create a thick, creamy layer on top of the cappuccino.
4. **Garnish (Optional):**
   - Dust the top of the foam with a sprinkle of cocoa powder or cinnamon if desired.
5. **Serve Immediately:**
   - Serve the cappuccino immediately while the foam is still fresh and creamy.

Tips:

- **Milk Choice:** Whole milk is preferred for its rich, creamy texture, but you can use any milk or milk alternative you like.
- **Milk Temperature:** Don't overheat the milk; it should be warm but not scalded, as overheating can affect the flavor.
- **Foam Texture:** Aim for a fine, velvety foam rather than large bubbles for the best texture.

Enjoy your perfectly crafted Cappuccino!

Latte

Ingredients:

- 1 shot (1 ounce) of freshly brewed espresso
- 8 ounces of milk
- Vanilla syrup or sweetener (optional)

Equipment:

- Espresso machine with a steam wand or a milk frother
- Coffee grinder (if using whole beans)

Instructions:

1. **Prepare the Espresso:**
    - Brew 1 shot (1 ounce) of espresso using an espresso machine or a stovetop espresso maker. Pour it into a pre-warmed latte cup.
2. **Steam the Milk:**
    - **With an Espresso Machine:** Fill a milk pitcher with 8 ounces of cold milk. Insert the steam wand into the pitcher and turn on the steam. Position the wand just below the surface of the milk and steam until the milk is warmed to about 150-160°F (65-70°C). Continue steaming until you achieve a creamy, velvety texture with minimal foam. You want more liquid milk than foam.
    - **With a Milk Frother:** If using a standalone milk frother, heat the milk according to the manufacturer's instructions and froth it lightly, aiming for a creamy texture rather than a lot of foam.
3. **Combine the Espresso and Milk:**
    - Gently swirl the steamed milk to combine any foam and liquid. Pour the steamed milk over the espresso, holding back the foam with a spoon if needed. Aim to create a smooth and creamy blend with a small amount of foam on top.
4. **Add Sweetener (Optional):**
    - If desired, add vanilla syrup or a sweetener of your choice to the espresso before pouring the milk.
5. **Serve Immediately:**
    - Serve the latte immediately while it's warm and creamy.

Tips:

- **Milk Choice:** Whole milk is typically used for its creaminess, but you can use any milk or milk alternative you prefer.
- **Milk Temperature:** Be careful not to overheat the milk; it should be warm and creamy, not scalded.
- **Foam Texture:** For a latte, aim for a smooth and creamy texture with only a thin layer of foam.

Enjoy your perfectly crafted Latte!

Macchiato

Ingredients:

- 1 shot (1 ounce) of freshly brewed espresso
- A small amount of steamed milk or milk foam (optional, depending on the style)

Equipment:

- Espresso machine
- Milk frother (if adding milk foam)

Instructions:

1. **Prepare the Espresso:**
   - Brew a shot (1 ounce) of espresso using an espresso machine or a stovetop espresso maker. Pour it into a small pre-warmed cup.
2. **Add the Milk (Optional):**
   - **Traditional Macchiato:** The traditional macchiato, also known as an "Espresso Macchiato," is simply an espresso with a small amount of milk or foam added. If desired, steam a small amount of milk (around 1 ounce) and spoon a small dollop of foam on top of the espresso. This adds just a touch of creaminess while preserving the strong espresso flavor.
   - **Latte Macchiato Style:** For a "Latte Macchiato" (a different version), steam and froth 4-6 ounces of milk and pour it into a glass, then add a shot of espresso on top. The espresso will create a distinct layer over the milk.
3. **Serve Immediately:**
   - Serve the macchiato immediately while it's fresh and hot.

Tips:

- **Espresso Quality:** Use freshly ground and well-roasted coffee beans for the best flavor.
- **Milk Texture:** If adding milk, aim for a small amount of froth. The focus of a macchiato is still on the espresso, with only a hint of milk or foam.
- **Customization:** Adjust the amount of milk or foam based on personal preference for a stronger or creamier taste.

Enjoy your Macchiato!

Americano

Ingredients:

- 1 shot (1 ounce) of freshly brewed espresso
- 6-8 ounces of hot water

Equipment:

- Espresso machine
- Kettle or hot water source

Instructions:

1. **Prepare the Espresso:**
   - Brew a shot (1 ounce) of espresso using an espresso machine or stovetop espresso maker. Pour it into a pre-warmed coffee cup.
2. **Heat the Water:**
   - Heat 6-8 ounces of water to just below boiling (about 190-200°F or 90-95°C). You can use a kettle or a hot water dispenser.
3. **Combine the Espresso and Water:**
   - Pour the hot water over the espresso. The amount of water can be adjusted based on your preference for a stronger or milder Americano. Generally, 6 ounces of water for a milder Americano or up to 8 ounces for a more diluted taste.
4. **Serve Immediately:**
   - Serve the Americano immediately while it's hot.

Tips:

- **Espresso Quality:** Use freshly ground and well-roasted coffee beans for the best flavor.
- **Water Temperature:** Ensure the water is hot but not boiling to avoid burning the coffee.
- **Adjusting Strength:** You can adjust the strength of the Americano by varying the amount of water used.

Enjoy your Americano!

Flat White

Ingredients:

- 1 shot (1 ounce) of freshly brewed espresso
- 4-6 ounces of milk

Equipment:

- Espresso machine with a steam wand
- Milk frother (if not using an espresso machine)
- Coffee grinder (if using whole beans)

Instructions:

1. **Prepare the Espresso:**
    - Brew a shot (1 ounce) of espresso using an espresso machine or stovetop espresso maker. Pour it into a pre-warmed cup.
2. **Steam the Milk:**
    - **With an Espresso Machine:** Fill a milk pitcher with 4-6 ounces of cold milk. Insert the steam wand into the pitcher and turn on the steam. Position the wand just below the surface of the milk and steam until the milk is warm (about 150-160°F or 65-70°C) and has a fine, velvety microfoam. Aim for a smooth, creamy texture with very little large foam.
    - **With a Milk Frother:** If using a standalone milk frother, heat the milk according to the manufacturer's instructions and froth it until you achieve a creamy, smooth microfoam.
3. **Combine the Espresso and Milk:**
    - Gently swirl the milk to incorporate the foam with the liquid. Pour the steamed milk over the espresso, aiming to create a smooth, creamy blend with a thin layer of microfoam on top. Pour slowly and steadily to achieve a consistent texture.
4. **Serve Immediately:**
    - Serve the Flat White immediately while it's fresh and hot.

Tips:

- **Milk Choice:** Whole milk is preferred for its rich, creamy texture, but you can use any milk or milk alternative you like.
- **Milk Texture:** For a Flat White, the milk should be steamed to a smooth, velvety texture with minimal foam, different from the thicker foam of a cappuccino.
- **Espresso Quality:** Use freshly ground coffee beans for the best flavor.

Enjoy your perfectly crafted Flat White!

Mocha

Ingredients:

- 1 shot (1 ounce) of freshly brewed espresso
- 6 ounces of milk
- 2 tablespoons of cocoa powder or chocolate syrup
- 1-2 tablespoons of sugar (optional, to taste)
- Whipped cream (optional, for topping)
- Chocolate shavings or cocoa powder (optional, for garnish)

Equipment:

- Espresso machine
- Milk frother or steam wand
- Small saucepan (if using cocoa powder)

Instructions:

1. **Prepare the Espresso:**
   - Brew a shot (1 ounce) of espresso using an espresso machine or stovetop espresso maker. Pour it into a pre-warmed coffee cup.
2. **Prepare the Chocolate Mixture:**
   - **Using Cocoa Powder:** In a small saucepan, combine 2 tablespoons of cocoa powder with 2 tablespoons of sugar (if using). Add a small amount of hot water (about 2 tablespoons) and stir until you form a smooth chocolate paste. Heat gently while stirring until warm and well combined.
   - **Using Chocolate Syrup:** Simply add 2 tablespoons of chocolate syrup directly to the espresso.
3. **Steam the Milk:**
   - **With an Espresso Machine:** Fill a milk pitcher with 6 ounces of cold milk. Insert the steam wand into the pitcher and turn on the steam. Position the wand just below the surface of the milk and steam until it reaches about 150-160°F (65-70°C) and has a creamy, velvety texture.
   - **With a Milk Frother:** If using a standalone milk frother, heat and froth the milk according to the manufacturer's instructions until it's creamy and warm.
4. **Combine Ingredients:**
   - Stir the chocolate mixture into the brewed espresso until well combined.
   - Pour the steamed milk over the chocolate-espresso mixture, holding back the foam with a spoon if needed. Gently stir to combine.
5. **Add Toppings (Optional):**
   - Top with a dollop of whipped cream and sprinkle with chocolate shavings or a dusting of cocoa powder if desired.
6. **Serve Immediately:**
   - Serve the Mocha immediately while it's warm and creamy.

Tips:

- **Chocolate Quality:** Use high-quality cocoa powder or chocolate syrup for the best flavor.
- **Sweetness:** Adjust the amount of sugar based on your taste preference.
- **Milk Choice:** Whole milk is typically preferred for a richer texture, but any milk or milk alternative can be used.

Enjoy your creamy, indulgent Mocha!

Cortado

Ingredients:

- 1 shot (1 ounce) of freshly brewed espresso
- 1 ounce of steamed milk

Equipment:

- Espresso machine with a steam wand
- Coffee grinder (if using whole beans)
- Milk frother (if not using an espresso machine)

Instructions:

1. **Prepare the Espresso:**
    - Brew a shot (1 ounce) of espresso using an espresso machine or stovetop espresso maker. Pour it into a pre-warmed small cup.
2. **Steam the Milk:**
    - **With an Espresso Machine:** Fill a milk pitcher with 1 ounce of cold milk. Insert the steam wand into the pitcher and turn on the steam. Position the wand just below the surface of the milk and steam until the milk is warm (about 150-160°F or 65-70°C) and has a silky, smooth texture with minimal foam.
    - **With a Milk Frother:** If using a standalone milk frother, heat and froth 1 ounce of milk according to the manufacturer's instructions until it's creamy and warm.
3. **Combine Espresso and Milk:**
    - Gently swirl the steamed milk to mix any foam with the liquid. Pour the steamed milk into the cup with the espresso, aiming to achieve a balanced blend of coffee and milk.
4. **Serve Immediately:**
    - Serve the Cortado immediately while it's hot and fresh.

Tips:

- **Milk Texture:** The Cortado should have a balanced ratio of espresso to milk, with a smooth, silky texture. The milk should be steamed but not overly foamy.
- **Espresso Quality:** Use freshly ground coffee beans for the best flavor.

Enjoy your perfectly balanced Cortado!

Affogato

Ingredients:

- 1 scoop of vanilla ice cream or gelato
- 1 shot (1 ounce) of freshly brewed espresso

Equipment:

- Espresso machine
- Ice cream scoop
- Coffee grinder (if using whole beans)

Instructions:

1. **Prepare the Espresso:**
   - Brew a shot (1 ounce) of espresso using an espresso machine or stovetop espresso maker.
2. **Scoop the Ice Cream:**
   - Place one scoop of vanilla ice cream or gelato into a pre-warmed dessert glass or bowl.
3. **Assemble the Affogato:**
   - Pour the freshly brewed espresso over the scoop of ice cream. The hot espresso will melt the ice cream slightly, creating a creamy, coffee-flavored sauce.
4. **Serve Immediately:**
   - Serve the Affogato immediately while the espresso is hot and the ice cream is still cold.

Tips:

- **Ice Cream Quality:** Use high-quality vanilla ice cream or gelato for the best flavor. You can experiment with other flavors like chocolate or caramel for a twist.
- **Espresso Strength:** Ensure the espresso is strong and freshly brewed to balance well with the ice cream.

Enjoy your deliciously simple Affogato!

Cold Brew Coffee

Ingredients:

- 1 cup coarsely ground coffee beans
- 4 cups cold, filtered water

Equipment:

- Large jar or pitcher
- Fine-mesh strainer or cheesecloth
- Coffee filter (optional, for extra clarity)

Instructions:

1. **Combine Coffee and Water:**
   - In a large jar or pitcher, combine 1 cup of coarsely ground coffee beans with 4 cups of cold, filtered water. Stir to ensure all the coffee grounds are saturated.
2. **Steep:**
   - Cover the jar or pitcher and let it steep at room temperature or in the refrigerator for 12-24 hours. The steeping time can vary based on how strong you like your coffee; longer steeping times generally produce a stronger brew.
3. **Strain:**
   - After steeping, strain the coffee concentrate through a fine-mesh strainer into another container. For a clearer brew, you can further strain it through a coffee filter or cheesecloth.
4. **Serve:**
   - Dilute the cold brew concentrate with water, milk, or a milk alternative to your taste preference (usually 1:1 ratio of concentrate to water or milk). Serve over ice.
5. **Store:**
   - Store any leftover cold brew concentrate in the refrigerator for up to 2 weeks.

Tips:

- **Grind Size:** Use coarsely ground coffee beans to avoid a bitter taste and make straining easier.
- **Strength:** Adjust the coffee-to-water ratio based on your preference for strength.
- **Flavor Variations:** You can infuse the cold brew with flavors like vanilla, cinnamon, or a splash of chocolate syrup for a unique twist.

Enjoy your smooth and refreshing Cold Brew Coffee!

Nitro Coffee

Ingredients:

- Cold brew coffee (prepared in advance)
- Nitrogen gas (typically from a nitrogen tank or nitro coffee infuser)

Equipment:

- Cold brew coffee (see recipe above for making)
- Nitro coffee infuser or a keg with a nitrogen gas system
- Coffee filter or fine-mesh strainer (for straining cold brew)

Instructions:

1. **Prepare Cold Brew Coffee:**
   - Brew a batch of cold brew coffee according to your preferred recipe (see Cold Brew Coffee recipe). Ensure the coffee is well-strained and chilled before use.
2. **Set Up Nitro System:**
   - If using a nitro coffee infuser, follow the manufacturer's instructions to fill it with the cold brew coffee. Attach the nitrogen gas canister or tank to the infuser according to the instructions.
3. **Infuse with Nitrogen:**
   - Charge the infuser with nitrogen gas. For most infusers, you'll need to shake the container gently to ensure the nitrogen is properly infused into the coffee. If using a keg system, you may need to let the coffee sit under nitrogen pressure for a few hours to fully infuse.
4. **Serve:**
   - Pour the nitro coffee from the infuser or keg into a glass. The nitrogen infusion should create a creamy, frothy head and a smooth, cascading effect as you pour. Serve immediately.
5. **Store (if applicable):**
   - If using a keg system, keep the nitro coffee refrigerated and under nitrogen pressure.

Tips:

- **Cold Brew Quality:** Start with a high-quality cold brew for the best flavor.
- **Nitrogen Infuser:** Ensure the nitro coffee infuser is clean and properly assembled to avoid any issues with infusion.
- **Serving:** Serve nitro coffee in a glass without ice, as it's already chilled and the nitrogen creates a frothy texture.

Enjoy your smooth, creamy Nitro Coffee with its signature frothy head and rich flavor!

Irish Coffee

Ingredients:

- 1 cup (8 ounces) hot brewed coffee
- 1.5 ounces Irish whiskey
- 1 tablespoon brown sugar (or to taste)
- Whipped cream (for topping)

Equipment:

- Heat-resistant glass or mug
- Coffee maker or French press
- Spoon

Instructions:

1. **Brew the Coffee:**
   - Brew a cup (8 ounces) of hot coffee using your preferred method (drip coffee maker, French press, etc.).
2. **Mix the Whiskey and Sugar:**
   - In a heat-resistant glass or mug, combine 1.5 ounces of Irish whiskey with 1 tablespoon of brown sugar. Stir until the sugar is fully dissolved.
3. **Add the Coffee:**
   - Pour the hot brewed coffee into the glass with the whiskey and sugar mixture. Stir well to combine.
4. **Top with Whipped Cream:**
   - Gently float a layer of whipped cream on top of the coffee. To achieve this, spoon the whipped cream over the back of a spoon so it rests on top of the coffee rather than mixing in.
5. **Serve Immediately:**
   - Serve the Irish Coffee immediately while hot, enjoying the contrast between the hot coffee and the cool, creamy topping.

Tips:

- **Whiskey Choice:** Use a good quality Irish whiskey for the best flavor.
- **Cream Texture:** For the perfect whipped cream, use heavy cream and beat until soft peaks form. Avoid overwhipping.
- **Serving Glass:** Use a glass with a handle to comfortably hold the hot beverage.

Enjoy your warm, comforting Irish Coffee!

Vietnamese Coffee

Ingredients:

- 2 tablespoons coarsely ground Vietnamese robusta coffee (or any strong coffee)
- 2-3 tablespoons sweetened condensed milk
- Hot water
- Ice cubes

Equipment:

- Vietnamese coffee filter (*phin*) or a drip coffee maker
- A heat-resistant cup or glass

Instructions:

1. **Prepare the Filter:**
   - Place 2-3 tablespoons of sweetened condensed milk in the bottom of your glass.
2. **Add the Coffee:**
   - Put the coffee grounds into the *phin* filter. Shake it a little to even out the grounds.
   - Place the *phin* on top of the glass with condensed milk.
3. **Brew the Coffee:**
   - Boil water and let it cool slightly (about 195°F to 205°F or 90°C to 96°C).
   - Pour a small amount of hot water over the coffee grounds to bloom them for about 30 seconds.
   - Then, pour in the rest of the hot water, filling the filter.
   - Cover the *phin* and let it drip slowly. This can take about 4-5 minutes.
4. **Mix and Chill:**
   - Once the coffee has finished dripping, stir the coffee and condensed milk together.
   - Fill a separate glass with ice cubes, then pour the coffee mixture over the ice.
5. **Serve:**
   - Stir well and enjoy your refreshing iced Vietnamese coffee!

Hot Vietnamese Coffee

Ingredients:

- 2 tablespoons coarsely ground Vietnamese robusta coffee (or any strong coffee)
- 2-3 tablespoons sweetened condensed milk
- Hot water

Equipment:

- Vietnamese coffee filter (*phin*) or a drip coffee maker
- A heat-resistant cup

Instructions:

1. **Prepare the Coffee:**
   - Place 2-3 tablespoons of sweetened condensed milk in the bottom of your heat-resistant cup.
2. **Add the Coffee:**
   - Place the coffee grounds into the *phin* filter. Shake it a little to even out the grounds.
   - Place the *phin* on top of the cup with condensed milk.
3. **Brew the Coffee:**
   - Boil water and let it cool slightly.
   - Pour a small amount of hot water over the coffee grounds to bloom them.
   - Then, pour in the rest of the hot water, filling the filter.
   - Cover the *phin* and let it drip slowly into the cup.
4. **Mix and Enjoy:**
   - Once the coffee has finished dripping, stir the coffee and condensed milk together.
   - Serve hot and enjoy!

Feel free to adjust the amount of condensed milk to match your preferred sweetness level. Enjoy making and drinking your Vietnamese coffee!

Turkish Coffee

Ingredients:

- 1 cup cold water (use the coffee cup you'll be drinking from for accurate measurement)
- 2-3 heaping teaspoons finely ground Turkish coffee (or very finely ground coffee)
- 1-2 teaspoons sugar (optional, adjust to taste)
- Cardamom (optional, for a traditional touch)

Equipment:

- A cezve (also known as an ibrik) or a small coffee pot
- A heat source (stove or open flame)
- A small spoon for stirring
- A demitasse cup (small coffee cup)

Instructions:

1. **Measure the Water:**
   - Pour cold water into the cezve, using the coffee cup you plan to use to ensure the right amount.
2. **Add Coffee:**
   - Add 2-3 heaping teaspoons of finely ground Turkish coffee to the cezve. Do not stir yet.
3. **Add Sugar (Optional):**
   - If you want your coffee sweetened, add 1-2 teaspoons of sugar. You can also add ground cardamom at this stage if you like its flavor.
4. **Stir:**
   - Stir the mixture gently to combine the coffee, sugar, and water. Make sure there are no coffee grounds floating on the surface.
5. **Heat:**
   - Place the cezve on a low heat. Allow the coffee to heat slowly without stirring. As it heats, you'll notice a frothy foam forming. Do not let it boil.
6. **Create Foam:**
   - When the foam starts to rise (just before boiling), remove the cezve from the heat. Skim off some of the foam and place it into your coffee cup.
7. **Finish Brewing:**
   - Return the cezve to the heat and let it rise again, then carefully pour the rest of the coffee into the cup. Pour slowly to avoid disturbing the coffee grounds settled at the bottom.
8. **Serve:**
   - Turkish coffee is typically enjoyed with a glass of water and sometimes a piece of Turkish delight or a small sweet treat.

Additional Tips:

- The grounds will settle at the bottom of the cup, so be careful not to drink the last sip, as it contains the thick coffee sludge.
- The coffee is traditionally enjoyed slowly and often accompanied by conversation.

Enjoy your Turkish coffee experience—it's as much about the ritual and flavor as it is about the coffee itself!

Espresso Martini

Ingredients:

- 1 1/2 oz (45 ml) vodka
- 1 oz (30 ml) coffee liqueur (e.g., Kahlúa)
- 1 oz (30 ml) freshly brewed espresso (cooled)
- 1/2 oz (15 ml) simple syrup (adjust to taste)
- Ice
- Coffee beans (for garnish)

Equipment:

- Cocktail shaker
- Strainer
- Martini glass

Instructions:

1. **Prepare the Espresso:**
   - Brew a shot of espresso and let it cool to room temperature. This is important so that it doesn't dilute the cocktail with heat.
2. **Mix the Ingredients:**
   - In a cocktail shaker, combine the vodka, coffee liqueur, cooled espresso, and simple syrup.
3. **Add Ice:**
   - Fill the shaker with ice, ensuring there's enough to chill and dilute the mixture properly.
4. **Shake:**
   - Shake vigorously for about 15-20 seconds. The goal is to create a frothy texture from the espresso, which will give the cocktail a nice crema on top.
5. **Strain:**
   - Strain the mixture into a chilled martini glass, using a fine mesh strainer if needed to remove any ice shards.
6. **Garnish:**
   - Garnish with a few coffee beans on top of the frothy surface.
7. **Serve:**
   - Serve immediately and enjoy the rich, creamy flavor of your Espresso Martini!

Tips:

- **Espresso Quality:** Use freshly brewed espresso for the best flavor. Pre-made or cold-brewed espresso can be used if you don't have an espresso machine, but fresh is ideal.
- **Simple Syrup:** You can adjust the amount of simple syrup depending on how sweet you like your cocktail. You can also use flavored syrups for a twist.

- **Shaking Technique:** Shaking the cocktail well is key to achieving the signature frothy crema on top.

This cocktail is perfect for a post-dinner drink or a stylish pick-me-up. Enjoy!

Coffee Tiramisu

Ingredients:

- **For the Coffee Mixture:**
    - 1 cup (240 ml) strong brewed coffee (cooled)
    - 1/4 cup (60 ml) coffee liqueur (e.g., Kahlúa) or Marsala wine (optional)
- **For the Mascarpone Cream:**
    - 6 large egg yolks
    - 3/4 cup (150 g) granulated sugar
    - 1 cup (240 ml) heavy cream
    - 8 oz (225 g) mascarpone cheese (room temperature)
    - 1 teaspoon vanilla extract
- **For Assembly:**
    - 24-30 ladyfingers (savoiardi), depending on the size
    - Unsweetened cocoa powder (for dusting)
    - Grated chocolate or shaved chocolate (optional, for garnish)

Instructions:

1. **Prepare the Coffee Mixture:**
    - Brew the coffee and let it cool to room temperature. Mix in the coffee liqueur or Marsala wine if using. Set aside.
2. **Make the Mascarpone Cream:**
    - In a medium saucepan, whisk together the egg yolks and granulated sugar. Heat the mixture over low heat, whisking constantly, until it thickens slightly and reaches 160°F (70°C). This will create a custard base.
    - Remove from heat and let cool to room temperature.
3. **Whip the Cream:**
    - In a separate bowl, whip the heavy cream until stiff peaks form.
4. **Combine Mascarpone and Custard:**
    - Gently fold the mascarpone cheese into the cooled custard mixture until smooth and combined.
5. **Incorporate Whipped Cream:**
    - Fold the whipped cream into the mascarpone-custard mixture gently until well combined and smooth. Be careful not to deflate the whipped cream.
6. **Assemble the Tiramisu:**
    - Briefly dip each ladyfinger into the coffee mixture, making sure they're coated but not soaked. Arrange a layer of dipped ladyfingers in the bottom of a serving dish (8x8-inch or similar).
    - Spread half of the mascarpone cream mixture over the ladyfingers.
    - Add another layer of dipped ladyfingers on top of the cream, followed by the remaining mascarpone cream.
7. **Chill:**

- Cover the dish with plastic wrap and refrigerate for at least 4 hours, or overnight for the best flavor and texture.
8. **Garnish:**
    - Before serving, dust the top of the tiramisu with unsweetened cocoa powder. You can also sprinkle grated or shaved chocolate for added decoration if desired.
9. **Serve:**
    - Serve chilled and enjoy!

Tips:

- **Egg Safety:** If you're concerned about using raw eggs, you can use pasteurized eggs or an egg substitute for the custard base.
- **Ladyfinger Tips:** Don't soak the ladyfingers too long; just a quick dip is enough to prevent them from becoming soggy.
- **Flavors:** Feel free to experiment with flavored liqueurs or extracts if you want to add a unique twist to the classic tiramisu flavor.

This coffee tiramisu is a crowd-pleaser that balances the bitterness of coffee with the sweetness of the mascarpone cream. Enjoy!

Coffee Crème Brûlée

Ingredients:

- **For the Custard:**
    - 2 cups (480 ml) heavy cream
    - 1 cup (240 ml) milk
    - 1/2 cup (100 g) granulated sugar
    - 1/4 cup (60 ml) strong brewed coffee (cooled)
    - 6 large egg yolks
    - 1 teaspoon vanilla extract
- **For the Topping:**
    - 1/4 cup (50 g) granulated sugar (for caramelizing)

Equipment:

- Ramekins (4 to 6, depending on size)
- Baking dish (for water bath)
- Whisk
- Fine-mesh sieve
- Kitchen torch or broiler (for caramelizing sugar)

Instructions:

1. **Preheat the Oven:**
    - Preheat your oven to 325°F (163°C).
2. **Prepare the Cream Mixture:**
    - In a medium saucepan, combine the heavy cream, milk, and granulated sugar. Heat over medium heat until the sugar dissolves and the mixture is hot but not boiling. Remove from heat.
    - Stir in the cooled brewed coffee and vanilla extract.
3. **Prepare the Egg Yolks:**
    - In a separate bowl, whisk the egg yolks until they are pale and slightly thickened.
4. **Combine Mixtures:**
    - Gradually add a small amount of the hot cream mixture into the egg yolks while whisking constantly to temper the eggs. Once combined, slowly whisk in the remaining cream mixture.
5. **Strain the Custard:**
    - Pour the custard mixture through a fine-mesh sieve into a clean bowl or measuring jug to remove any curdled bits and ensure a smooth custard.
6. **Prepare the Ramekins:**
    - Place your ramekins in a baking dish. Divide the custard mixture evenly among the ramekins.
7. **Bake:**

- Fill the baking dish with hot water until it reaches halfway up the sides of the ramekins (this is your water bath). Carefully place the baking dish in the oven.
- Bake for 40-50 minutes, or until the custards are set but still slightly jiggly in the center.

8. **Cool and Chill:**
   - Remove the ramekins from the water bath and let them cool to room temperature. Once cool, cover and refrigerate for at least 2 hours, or up to 2 days.
9. **Caramelize the Sugar:**
   - Just before serving, sprinkle an even layer of granulated sugar over the top of each custard. Use a kitchen torch to melt and caramelize the sugar until it forms a golden, crispy layer. If you don't have a torch, you can place the ramekins under a broiler for a minute or two, watching closely to avoid burning.
10. **Serve:**
    - Allow the caramelized sugar to cool and harden before serving.

Tips:

- **Coffee Strength:** Adjust the strength of your coffee to taste. For a more intense coffee flavor, use a stronger brew.
- **Avoid Boiling:** When heating the cream mixture, avoid boiling as it can curdle the cream.
- **Torch Technique:** If using a kitchen torch, keep it moving to evenly caramelize the sugar without burning it.

This Coffee Crème Brûlée combines the luxurious, creamy texture of traditional crème brûlée with a robust coffee flavor, making it a perfect dessert for coffee lovers. Enjoy!

Coffee Gelato

Ingredients:

- 1 cup (240 ml) whole milk
- 1 cup (240 ml) heavy cream
- 1/2 cup (100 g) granulated sugar
- 1/2 cup (120 ml) strong brewed coffee (cooled)
- 4 large egg yolks
- 1 teaspoon vanilla extract (optional)

Equipment:

- Ice cream maker
- Saucepan
- Whisk
- Mixing bowl
- Fine-mesh sieve

Instructions:

1. **Prepare the Coffee:**
   - Brew a strong cup of coffee and let it cool to room temperature.
2. **Heat the Milk and Cream:**
   - In a medium saucepan, combine the whole milk and heavy cream. Heat over medium heat until the mixture is hot but not boiling.
3. **Whisk the Egg Yolks:**
   - In a separate bowl, whisk together the egg yolks and granulated sugar until the mixture is pale and slightly thickened.
4. **Temper the Egg Yolks:**
   - Gradually add a small amount of the hot milk and cream mixture into the egg yolks while whisking constantly. This helps to temper the eggs and prevent them from curdling.
5. **Combine and Cook:**
   - Pour the egg yolk mixture back into the saucepan with the remaining milk and cream. Cook over medium heat, stirring constantly with a wooden spoon or heatproof spatula, until the mixture thickens slightly and reaches 170-175°F (77-80°C). Be careful not to let it boil.
6. **Add Coffee and Strain:**
   - Remove the saucepan from heat and stir in the cooled brewed coffee. If using, add the vanilla extract.
   - Pour the mixture through a fine-mesh sieve into a clean bowl to remove any cooked egg bits and ensure a smooth texture.
7. **Cool the Mixture:**

- Allow the mixture to cool to room temperature. Once cooled, cover the bowl with plastic wrap and refrigerate for at least 4 hours or overnight to chill thoroughly.
8. **Churn the Gelato:**
   - Pour the chilled mixture into an ice cream maker and churn according to the manufacturer's instructions. This usually takes about 20-30 minutes.
9. **Freeze:**
   - Transfer the churned gelato to an airtight container and freeze for at least 2 hours to firm up.
10. **Serve:**
    - Scoop the coffee gelato into bowls or cones and enjoy!

Tips:

- **Coffee Strength:** Adjust the strength of your coffee based on your preference. A stronger brew will give you a more intense coffee flavor.
- **Texture:** If you don't have an ice cream maker, you can still make gelato by periodically stirring the mixture as it freezes to break up ice crystals.
- **Storage:** Store gelato in an airtight container in the freezer to keep it fresh. It's best enjoyed within a couple of weeks.

Coffee gelato is a smooth and indulgent dessert that combines the rich flavors of coffee with the creamy texture of gelato. Enjoy making and savoring this delicious treat!

Coffee Cheesecake

Ingredients:

- **For the Crust:**
    - 1 1/2 cups (150 g) graham cracker crumbs (or digestive biscuit crumbs)
    - 1/4 cup (50 g) granulated sugar
    - 1/2 cup (115 g) unsalted butter, melted
- **For the Filling:**
    - 4 (8 oz each) (225 g each) cream cheese blocks, softened
    - 1 cup (200 g) granulated sugar
    - 1 cup (240 ml) sour cream
    - 1 cup (240 ml) heavy cream
    - 1/2 cup (120 ml) strong brewed coffee (cooled)
    - 4 large eggs
    - 1 teaspoon vanilla extract
    - 1 tablespoon all-purpose flour (optional, helps stabilize the filling)
- **For the Topping (Optional):**
    - Whipped cream
    - Chocolate shavings or cocoa powder

Equipment:

- 9-inch (23 cm) springform pan
- Mixing bowls
- Electric mixer or stand mixer
- Baking pan (for water bath)
- Aluminum foil (for wrapping the pan)
- Oven

Instructions:

1. **Preheat Oven:**
    - Preheat your oven to 325°F (163°C).
2. **Prepare the Crust:**
    - In a medium bowl, combine the graham cracker crumbs, granulated sugar, and melted butter. Mix until the crumbs are evenly coated.
    - Press the mixture firmly into the bottom of a 9-inch (23 cm) springform pan to form an even layer. Use the back of a spoon or the bottom of a glass to press it down firmly.
3. **Bake the Crust:**
    - Bake the crust in the preheated oven for 10 minutes. Remove from the oven and let it cool while you prepare the filling.
4. **Prepare the Filling:**

- In a large mixing bowl, beat the softened cream cheese with an electric mixer until smooth and creamy.
- Gradually add the granulated sugar and continue beating until well combined and smooth.
- Add the sour cream and beat until fully incorporated.
- Mix in the heavy cream and cooled coffee, beating until the mixture is smooth.
- Add the eggs one at a time, mixing well after each addition. If using, mix in the flour.
- Finally, add the vanilla extract and mix until just combined.

5. **Prepare the Springform Pan:**
   - Wrap the bottom of the springform pan with aluminum foil to prevent water from seeping in during the water bath.

6. **Bake the Cheesecake:**
   - Pour the filling over the cooled crust in the springform pan.
   - Place the springform pan in a larger baking pan and add hot water to the outer pan until it reaches halfway up the sides of the springform pan (this is your water bath).
   - Bake the cheesecake for 60-70 minutes, or until the edges are set and the center is slightly jiggly. The cheesecake will continue to firm up as it cools.

7. **Cool and Chill:**
   - Turn off the oven and crack the oven door slightly. Let the cheesecake cool in the oven for 1 hour.
   - Remove the cheesecake from the water bath and refrigerate for at least 4 hours, or overnight, to chill and set.

8. **Serve:**
   - Before serving, top with whipped cream and garnish with chocolate shavings or a dusting of cocoa powder if desired.

Tips:

- **Prevent Cracks:** To prevent cracks, avoid overmixing the batter and make sure the cheesecake is baked in a water bath.
- **Flavor Adjustment:** Adjust the coffee strength according to your preference. For a stronger coffee flavor, use a more concentrated brew.
- **Cheese Texture:** Ensure the cream cheese is softened to room temperature before mixing to avoid lumps.

This coffee cheesecake is a rich and satisfying dessert, perfect for coffee lovers and cheesecake enthusiasts alike. Enjoy!

Coffee Caramel Sauce

Ingredients:

- 1 cup (200 g) granulated sugar
- 6 tablespoons (85 g) unsalted butter, cut into pieces
- 1/2 cup (120 ml) heavy cream
- 1/2 cup (120 ml) strong brewed coffee (hot)
- 1/4 teaspoon salt (optional, for added flavor)

Equipment:

- Medium saucepan
- Wooden spoon or heat-resistant spatula
- Heatproof jar or container for storing

Instructions:

1. **Cook the Sugar:**
    - In a medium saucepan, heat the granulated sugar over medium heat. Stir constantly with a wooden spoon or heat-resistant spatula to ensure the sugar melts evenly and doesn't burn.
    - The sugar will start to clump and then turn into a liquid. Continue to stir until the sugar is completely melted and has turned a deep amber color.
2. **Add the Butter:**
    - Carefully add the butter pieces to the melted sugar. The mixture will bubble vigorously, so be cautious. Stir continuously until the butter is completely melted and incorporated.
3. **Incorporate the Cream:**
    - Gradually pour in the heavy cream while stirring. The mixture will bubble up again, but keep stirring until smooth and well combined.
4. **Add Coffee and Salt:**
    - Slowly add the hot brewed coffee to the mixture while stirring. The coffee will blend with the caramel, creating a rich, coffee-infused sauce. Stir until smooth.
    - If desired, add a pinch of salt to enhance the flavors.
5. **Cool and Store:**
    - Remove the saucepan from heat and let the caramel sauce cool for a few minutes. It will thicken as it cools.
    - Transfer the sauce to a heatproof jar or container. Once cooled to room temperature, store it in the refrigerator. It can be reheated in the microwave or on the stove if needed.
6. **Serve:**
    - Drizzle the coffee caramel sauce over your favorite desserts, such as ice cream, cheesecake, or pancakes. Enjoy!

Tips:

- **Consistency:** If the caramel sauce is too thick after cooling, gently reheat it and stir in a little extra cream to reach the desired consistency.
- **Coffee Strength:** Adjust the strength of the coffee based on your taste preferences. For a stronger coffee flavor, use a more concentrated brew.
- **Storage:** Store the caramel sauce in an airtight container in the refrigerator for up to 2 weeks. Reheat gently before use.

This coffee caramel sauce is a versatile and flavorful topping that adds a delightful twist to many desserts. Enjoy!

Coffee Brownies

Ingredients:

- **For the Brownies:**
    - 1 cup (225 g) unsalted butter
    - 1 cup (200 g) granulated sugar
    - 2 large eggs
    - 1 cup (200 g) packed brown sugar
    - 1/2 cup (120 ml) strong brewed coffee (cooled)
    - 1 teaspoon vanilla extract
    - 1 cup (125 g) all-purpose flour
    - 1/2 cup (50 g) unsweetened cocoa powder
    - 1/2 teaspoon baking powder
    - 1/4 teaspoon salt
    - 1/2 cup (100 g) semi-sweet chocolate chips (optional)
- **For the Coffee Glaze (Optional):**
    - 1/2 cup (60 g) powdered sugar
    - 1-2 tablespoons strong brewed coffee

Equipment:

- 9x9-inch (23x23 cm) baking pan
- Parchment paper (for lining)
- Mixing bowls
- Whisk
- Rubber spatula
- Measuring cups and spoons

Instructions:

1. **Preheat Oven:**
    - Preheat your oven to 350°F (175°C). Line a 9x9-inch (23x23 cm) baking pan with parchment paper, leaving some overhang for easy removal.
2. **Melt Butter and Mix Sugars:**
    - In a medium saucepan, melt the butter over low heat. Remove from heat and stir in granulated sugar and brown sugar until well combined.
3. **Add Eggs and Coffee:**
    - Beat in the eggs, one at a time, until fully incorporated. Stir in the cooled coffee and vanilla extract.
4. **Mix Dry Ingredients:**
    - In a separate bowl, whisk together the flour, cocoa powder, baking powder, and salt.
5. **Combine and Add Chocolate Chips:**

- Gradually add the dry ingredients to the wet ingredients, mixing until just combined. Fold in the chocolate chips, if using.
6. **Bake:**
    - Pour the batter into the prepared baking pan and spread it evenly.
    - Bake in the preheated oven for 25-30 minutes, or until a toothpick inserted into the center comes out with a few moist crumbs. Avoid overbaking to keep the brownies fudgy.
7. **Cool and Optional Glaze:**
    - Let the brownies cool in the pan on a wire rack.
    - If making the coffee glaze, whisk together the powdered sugar and brewed coffee until smooth and drizzle over the cooled brownies.
8. **Serve:**
    - Once the glaze is set (if used), cut the brownies into squares and serve.

Tips:

- **Coffee Strength:** Adjust the strength of the coffee to your preference. A stronger coffee will give a more pronounced coffee flavor.
- **Storage:** Store brownies in an airtight container at room temperature for up to 5 days or refrigerate for longer freshness.
- **Mix-ins:** Feel free to add nuts, toffee bits, or other mix-ins to the brownie batter for extra texture and flavor.

Enjoy these coffee brownies with a cup of coffee or as a delicious treat on their own!

Coffee Macarons

Ingredients:

- **For the Macaron Shells:**
    - 1 3/4 cups (200 g) almond flour
    - 1 1/2 cups (190 g) powdered sugar
    - 3 large egg whites
    - 1/4 teaspoon cream of tartar
    - 1/2 cup (100 g) granulated sugar
    - 1 tablespoon instant coffee granules (or finely ground espresso)
- **For the Coffee Buttercream Filling:**
    - 1/2 cup (115 g) unsalted butter, softened
    - 1 cup (120 g) powdered sugar
    - 1 tablespoon instant coffee granules (or finely ground espresso)
    - 1 tablespoon heavy cream
    - 1 teaspoon vanilla extract (optional)

Equipment:

- Baking sheets
- Parchment paper or silicone baking mats
- Stand mixer or electric hand mixer
- Sifter
- Piping bags with round tips
- Offset spatula

Instructions:

1. **Prepare the Coffee:**
    - Dissolve the instant coffee granules in a small amount of hot water and let it cool completely. This will be used in both the shells and the filling.
2. **Prepare the Baking Sheets:**
    - Preheat your oven to 300°F (150°C). Line baking sheets with parchment paper or silicone baking mats.
3. **Sift Dry Ingredients:**
    - Sift the almond flour and powdered sugar together into a large bowl. Set aside.
4. **Whip Egg Whites:**
    - In a clean mixing bowl, add the egg whites and cream of tartar. Using a stand mixer or electric hand mixer, whip the egg whites on medium speed until they become frothy.
    - Gradually add the granulated sugar while continuing to whip until stiff peaks form and the meringue is glossy.
5. **Incorporate Coffee:**

- Gently fold the dissolved coffee into the meringue. Be careful not to deflate the meringue.
6. **Combine Dry Ingredients:**
   - Gradually fold the sifted almond flour and powdered sugar mixture into the meringue using a spatula. The batter should be smooth and flow like lava, with a ribbon-like consistency.
7. **Pipe the Macarons:**
   - Transfer the macaron batter to a piping bag fitted with a round tip. Pipe small, round circles (about 1.5 inches or 4 cm in diameter) onto the prepared baking sheets, spacing them about 1 inch apart.
8. **Rest the Shells:**
   - Tap the baking sheets gently on the counter to release air bubbles and smooth the tops. Let the macarons sit at room temperature for 30-60 minutes, or until a skin forms on the surface and they are no longer tacky to the touch.
9. **Bake:**
   - Bake the macarons in the preheated oven for 15-20 minutes, or until the shells are firm and easily lift off the parchment paper. Let them cool completely on the baking sheets.
10. **Prepare the Coffee Buttercream Filling:**
    - In a mixing bowl, beat the softened butter until creamy.
    - Gradually add the powdered sugar and mix until smooth.
    - Dissolve the instant coffee granules in the heavy cream and add to the butter mixture. Beat until combined and the filling is light and fluffy. Add vanilla extract if desired.
11. **Assemble the Macarons:**
    - Pair the macaron shells of similar size. Pipe a small amount of coffee buttercream onto the flat side of one shell, then sandwich with the other shell.
12. **Mature the Macarons:**
    - For the best flavor and texture, let the assembled macarons mature in the refrigerator for at least 24 hours. This allows the flavors to meld and the filling to soften the shells.
13. **Serve:**
    - Allow the macarons to come to room temperature before serving. Enjoy!

Tips:

- **Sifting:** Sift the almond flour and powdered sugar to ensure a smooth macaron texture and avoid lumps.
- **Meringue:** Make sure your mixing bowl and beaters are completely clean and free of grease to achieve the right meringue consistency.
- **Resting:** Properly resting the macarons before baking helps them develop their signature "feet" and prevents cracking.

These coffee macarons are perfect for a sophisticated treat or to impress guests at a special occasion. Enjoy!

Coffee Granita

Ingredients:

- 2 cups (480 ml) strong brewed coffee (cooled)
- 1/2 cup (100 g) granulated sugar
- 1/4 cup (60 ml) water
- 1 teaspoon vanilla extract (optional)
- Whipped cream (optional, for serving)

Instructions:

1. **Prepare the Coffee:**
    - Brew a strong cup of coffee and let it cool to room temperature. You can use espresso or a strong coffee brew, depending on your preference.
2. **Make the Syrup:**
    - In a small saucepan, combine the granulated sugar and water. Heat over medium heat, stirring occasionally, until the sugar is completely dissolved. Remove from heat and let cool.
3. **Combine Ingredients:**
    - In a mixing bowl, combine the cooled coffee, sugar syrup, and vanilla extract (if using). Stir well to combine.
4. **Freeze the Mixture:**
    - Pour the mixture into a shallow, freezer-safe dish. A metal or glass dish works well.
5. **Scrape the Granita:**
    - After about 1-2 hours, or once the mixture starts to freeze around the edges, use a fork to scrape and stir the ice crystals. Return to the freezer.
    - Continue to scrape and stir the granita every 30 minutes or so, for a total of about 3-4 hours, until the mixture is fully frozen and has a fluffy, granular texture.
6. **Serve:**
    - Once the granita is ready, use a fork to fluff it up before serving. Spoon it into glasses or bowls.
7. **Optional Topping:**
    - Top with a dollop of whipped cream if desired for added indulgence.

Tips:

- **Coffee Strength:** Adjust the strength of your coffee based on your taste preference. A stronger coffee will give a more pronounced flavor.
- **Texture:** Scraping the granita every 30 minutes helps achieve the perfect fluffy texture. If you don't have time to scrape frequently, it will still be delicious but might be more icy than fluffy.
- **Sweetness:** You can adjust the amount of sugar in the syrup to taste. If you prefer a less sweet granita, reduce the sugar amount.

Coffee granita is a simple yet sophisticated dessert that captures the essence of coffee in a cool, refreshing form. Enjoy!

Coffee Panna Cotta

Ingredients:

- 1 cup (240 ml) heavy cream
- 1 cup (240 ml) whole milk
- 1/2 cup (100 g) granulated sugar
- 1/2 cup (120 ml) strong brewed coffee (cooled)
- 1 envelope (2 1/4 teaspoons) unflavored gelatin
- 3 tablespoons cold water
- 1 teaspoon vanilla extract (optional)

Instructions:

1. **Prepare Gelatin:**
   - In a small bowl, sprinkle the gelatin over the cold water. Let it sit for about 5 minutes to bloom (soften).
2. **Heat Cream and Milk:**
   - In a medium saucepan, combine the heavy cream, whole milk, and granulated sugar. Heat over medium heat, stirring occasionally, until the sugar is completely dissolved and the mixture is hot but not boiling.
3. **Dissolve Gelatin:**
   - Once the cream mixture is hot, remove it from the heat. Add the bloomed gelatin and stir until completely dissolved.
4. **Add Coffee and Vanilla:**
   - Stir in the cooled brewed coffee and vanilla extract (if using). Mix until well combined.
5. **Pour into Molds:**
   - Pour the mixture into individual serving glasses or ramekins.
6. **Chill:**
   - Refrigerate for at least 4 hours, or until the panna cotta is set and firm to the touch.
7. **Serve:**
   - Once set, the panna cotta can be served directly from the glasses or ramekins. You can garnish with a sprinkle of cocoa powder, a few coffee beans, or a dollop of whipped cream if desired.

Tips:

- **Gelatin:** Ensure that the gelatin is completely dissolved to avoid lumps. If there are any lumps, you can strain the mixture before pouring it into the molds.
- **Coffee Strength:** Use strong coffee for a more pronounced coffee flavor. Adjust the strength according to your taste preferences.

- **Molds:** If you want to unmold the panna cotta, lightly oil the inside of the molds before pouring in the mixture. To release the panna cotta, briefly dip the bottoms of the molds in warm water.

Coffee panna cotta is a delightful combination of creamy and coffee flavors, offering a sophisticated and satisfying dessert experience. Enjoy!

Coffee Truffles

Ingredients:

- 1 cup (240 ml) heavy cream
- 8 oz (225 g) semi-sweet or dark chocolate, chopped
- 2 tablespoons instant coffee granules or finely ground espresso
- 2 tablespoons unsalted butter
- Cocoa powder, finely ground coffee, or melted chocolate (for rolling)

Instructions:

1. **Heat the Cream:**
   - In a small saucepan, heat the heavy cream over medium heat until it starts to simmer. Do not let it boil.
2. **Prepare the Chocolate:**
   - Place the chopped chocolate in a heatproof bowl. Add the instant coffee granules or finely ground espresso to the bowl.
3. **Combine Cream and Chocolate:**
   - Pour the hot cream over the chopped chocolate. Let it sit for 1-2 minutes to allow the chocolate to melt.
   - Add the unsalted butter to the mixture. Stir gently until the chocolate is fully melted and the mixture is smooth and glossy.
4. **Chill the Mixture:**
   - Cover the bowl with plastic wrap and refrigerate the chocolate mixture for about 1-2 hours, or until it is firm enough to scoop.
5. **Form the Truffles:**
   - Once the mixture is firm, use a small cookie scoop or a teaspoon to scoop out small amounts of the mixture. Roll them quickly between your hands to form smooth balls. Work swiftly to avoid melting the mixture with your hands.
6. **Coat the Truffles:**
   - Roll the truffles in cocoa powder, finely ground coffee, or dip them in melted chocolate. If rolling in cocoa powder or coffee, place the truffles in a small bowl with the coating and gently toss until covered.
7. **Chill Again:**
   - Place the coated truffles on a parchment-lined tray and refrigerate for another 30 minutes to set.
8. **Serve:**
   - Once set, serve the truffles at room temperature. They can be stored in an airtight container in the refrigerator for up to 2 weeks.

Tips:

- **Chocolate Quality:** Use high-quality chocolate for the best flavor and texture.

- **Flavor Variations:** You can add a splash of liqueur (such as Kahlúa) to the ganache for an extra kick, or incorporate flavor extracts like vanilla or almond.
- **Coating Options:** Besides cocoa powder and ground coffee, you can also roll the truffles in chopped nuts, sprinkles, or even drizzle with additional melted chocolate.

Coffee truffles are a luxurious treat that blends the deep flavors of chocolate and coffee, perfect for gifting or enjoying with a cup of coffee. Enjoy!

Coffee Banana Bread

Ingredients:

- 1/2 cup (115 g) unsalted butter, softened
- 1 cup (200 g) granulated sugar
- 2 large eggs
- 1 cup (240 ml) strong brewed coffee (cooled)
- 3 ripe bananas, mashed (about 1 1/2 cups)
- 1 teaspoon vanilla extract
- 1 1/2 cups (190 g) all-purpose flour
- 1 teaspoon baking powder
- 1/2 teaspoon baking soda
- 1/2 teaspoon salt
- 1/2 teaspoon ground cinnamon (optional)
- 1/2 cup (60 g) chopped walnuts or chocolate chips (optional)

Equipment:

- 9x5-inch (23x13 cm) loaf pan
- Parchment paper (for lining)
- Mixing bowls
- Electric mixer or whisk
- Rubber spatula

Instructions:

1. **Preheat Oven:**
   - Preheat your oven to 350°F (175°C). Grease and flour a 9x5-inch (23x13 cm) loaf pan, or line it with parchment paper for easy removal.
2. **Mix Wet Ingredients:**
   - In a large bowl, cream together the softened butter and granulated sugar until light and fluffy.
   - Beat in the eggs, one at a time, until fully incorporated.
   - Add the cooled coffee, mashed bananas, and vanilla extract. Mix well until combined.
3. **Combine Dry Ingredients:**
   - In a separate bowl, whisk together the flour, baking powder, baking soda, salt, and ground cinnamon (if using).
4. **Mix Dry into Wet:**
   - Gradually add the dry ingredients to the wet ingredients, mixing until just combined. Be careful not to overmix.
   - Fold in the chopped walnuts or chocolate chips if using.
5. **Pour and Bake:**
   - Pour the batter into the prepared loaf pan, spreading it evenly.

- Bake in the preheated oven for 60-70 minutes, or until a toothpick inserted into the center of the loaf comes out clean.
6. **Cool:**
    - Allow the banana bread to cool in the pan for 10 minutes, then transfer it to a wire rack to cool completely before slicing.
7. **Serve:**
    - Enjoy your coffee banana bread plain, or with a pat of butter or a drizzle of honey.

Tips:

- **Bananas:** Make sure the bananas are very ripe for the best flavor and sweetness.
- **Coffee Strength:** Adjust the strength of the coffee based on your preference. A stronger coffee will give a more pronounced coffee flavor.
- **Mix-ins:** Feel free to add other mix-ins like dried fruit or a swirl of Nutella for added flavor and texture.
- **Storage:** Store the banana bread in an airtight container at room temperature for up to 5 days, or freeze for up to 3 months.

Coffee banana bread is a delightful treat that pairs well with a cup of coffee or tea, offering a delicious combination of flavors and textures. Enjoy!

Coffee Almond Cake

Ingredients:

- **For the Cake:**
    - 1 cup (100 g) almond flour (or finely ground almonds)
    - 1 cup (125 g) all-purpose flour
    - 1 cup (200 g) granulated sugar
    - 1/2 cup (115 g) unsalted butter, softened
    - 1/2 cup (120 ml) strong brewed coffee (cooled)
    - 1/2 cup (120 ml) milk
    - 3 large eggs
    - 1 teaspoon vanilla extract
    - 1 tablespoon baking powder
    - 1/4 teaspoon salt
    - 1/2 cup (50 g) sliced almonds (for topping)
- **For the Coffee Glaze (optional):**
    - 1/2 cup (60 g) powdered sugar
    - 1-2 tablespoons strong brewed coffee (cooled)

Instructions:

1. **Preheat Oven:**
    - Preheat your oven to 350°F (175°C). Grease and flour an 8-inch (20 cm) round cake pan or line it with parchment paper.
2. **Prepare the Cake Batter:**
    - In a medium bowl, sift together the all-purpose flour, baking powder, and salt. Set aside.
    - In a large bowl, cream together the softened butter and granulated sugar until light and fluffy.
    - Beat in the eggs, one at a time, until fully incorporated.
    - Mix in the vanilla extract and the cooled brewed coffee.
    - Gradually add the dry ingredients to the wet ingredients, alternating with the milk. Begin and end with the dry ingredients. Mix until just combined.
    - Fold in the almond flour (or finely ground almonds).
3. **Pour and Bake:**
    - Pour the batter into the prepared cake pan, smoothing the top with a spatula.
    - Sprinkle the sliced almonds evenly over the top of the batter.
    - Bake in the preheated oven for 30-35 minutes, or until a toothpick inserted into the center of the cake comes out clean.
4. **Cool and Glaze (optional):**
    - Allow the cake to cool in the pan for 10 minutes before transferring it to a wire rack to cool completely.
    - If making the coffee glaze, whisk together the powdered sugar and brewed coffee until smooth. Drizzle the glaze over the cooled cake.

5. **Serve:**
    - Slice and serve the cake plain, or with a dollop of whipped cream or a scoop of vanilla ice cream.

Tips:

- **Coffee Strength:** Adjust the strength of the coffee to your taste. A stronger coffee will impart a more pronounced flavor.
- **Almond Flour:** If you prefer a more pronounced almond flavor, use a bit more almond flour or finely ground almonds.
- **Storage:** Store the cake in an airtight container at room temperature for up to 3 days, or refrigerate for up to a week. It can also be frozen for up to 3 months.

Coffee almond cake offers a delightful blend of flavors and textures, making it a perfect choice for coffee lovers and cake enthusiasts alike. Enjoy!

Coffee Ice Cream Sundae

Ingredients:

- **For the Sundae:**
    - 2-3 scoops of coffee ice cream (store-bought or homemade)
    - 1/4 cup (60 ml) espresso or strong brewed coffee (cooled)
    - 1/4 cup (60 ml) chocolate sauce or hot fudge (store-bought or homemade)
    - Whipped cream
    - Chocolate shavings or sprinkles (optional)
    - Crushed nuts or biscotti (optional)
- **For Homemade Chocolate Sauce (Optional):**
    - 1/2 cup (120 ml) heavy cream
    - 1/2 cup (90 g) semi-sweet chocolate chips
    - 1 tablespoon light corn syrup or honey (optional, for shine)

Instructions:

1. **Prepare the Chocolate Sauce (if making homemade):**
    - In a small saucepan, heat the heavy cream over medium heat until it begins to simmer.
    - Remove from heat and add the chocolate chips. Let sit for 1-2 minutes to soften.
    - Stir until the chocolate is completely melted and the sauce is smooth. Add the corn syrup or honey if using. Let the sauce cool slightly before using.
2. **Assemble the Sundae:**
    - Scoop 2-3 scoops of coffee ice cream into a serving bowl or dish.
    - Drizzle the cooled espresso or strong brewed coffee over the ice cream. You can adjust the amount based on how strong you want the coffee flavor.
    - Spoon the chocolate sauce or hot fudge over the top of the ice cream.
    - Add a generous dollop of whipped cream.
3. **Add Toppings:**
    - Garnish with chocolate shavings, sprinkles, or crushed nuts if desired.
    - For extra crunch and flavor, you can also add pieces of biscotti.
4. **Serve:**
    - Serve immediately with a spoon or an ice cream scoop.

Tips:

- **Coffee Ice Cream:** If you're making your own coffee ice cream, make sure it's well-chilled and slightly softened before serving for easier scooping.
- **Coffee Strength:** Adjust the strength of the coffee or espresso to your taste preference. A stronger coffee will give a more pronounced flavor.
- **Storage:** Store any leftover chocolate sauce in an airtight container in the refrigerator. Reheat gently before using.

This coffee ice cream sundae is a delicious and sophisticated treat that combines the flavors of coffee, chocolate, and cream. It's perfect for coffee lovers and makes a wonderful dessert for any occasion. Enjoy!

Coffee Scones

Ingredients:

- **For the Scones:**
    - 2 1/4 cups (280 g) all-purpose flour
    - 1/4 cup (50 g) granulated sugar
    - 1 tablespoon baking powder
    - 1/2 teaspoon salt
    - 1/2 cup (115 g) unsalted butter, cold and cut into small cubes
    - 1/2 cup (120 ml) heavy cream
    - 1/4 cup (60 ml) strong brewed coffee (cooled)
    - 1 large egg
    - 1 teaspoon vanilla extract (optional)
- **For the Coffee Glaze (optional):**
    - 1/2 cup (60 g) powdered sugar
    - 1-2 tablespoons strong brewed coffee (cooled)

Instructions:

1. **Preheat Oven:**
    - Preheat your oven to 400°F (200°C). Line a baking sheet with parchment paper or lightly grease it.
2. **Prepare Dry Ingredients:**
    - In a large mixing bowl, whisk together the flour, sugar, baking powder, and salt.
3. **Cut in the Butter:**
    - Add the cold butter cubes to the dry ingredients. Use a pastry cutter, fork, or your fingers to cut the butter into the flour mixture until it resembles coarse crumbs with pea-sized pieces of butter.
4. **Combine Wet Ingredients:**
    - In a separate bowl, whisk together the heavy cream, cooled coffee, egg, and vanilla extract (if using).
5. **Mix Wet and Dry Ingredients:**
    - Pour the wet ingredients into the dry ingredients. Stir until just combined. The dough will be slightly sticky.
6. **Shape and Cut:**
    - Turn the dough out onto a floured surface. Gently knead it a few times to bring it together, then pat it into a 1-inch thick circle.
    - Use a sharp knife or a pizza cutter to cut the dough into 8 wedges, or use a round cutter to make circles if you prefer.
7. **Bake:**
    - Place the scones on the prepared baking sheet, spacing them about 1 inch apart.
    - Bake in the preheated oven for 15-20 minutes, or until the scones are golden brown and a toothpick inserted into the center comes out clean.
8. **Cool and Glaze (optional):**

- Allow the scones to cool slightly on a wire rack.
- If making the coffee glaze, whisk together the powdered sugar and brewed coffee until smooth. Drizzle the glaze over the warm scones.

9. **Serve:**
    - Enjoy the scones warm or at room temperature with a cup of coffee or tea.

Tips:

- **Butter:** Make sure the butter is cold to achieve a flaky texture. You can even chill the flour mixture and butter before starting to keep everything cold.
- **Mixing:** Don't overmix the dough to avoid dense scones. Mix until the dough just comes together.
- **Coffee Strength:** Adjust the amount of coffee to your taste. You can use espresso for a stronger coffee flavor or a lighter brew for a milder taste.
- **Storage:** Store leftover scones in an airtight container at room temperature for up to 3 days, or freeze for up to 2 months.

These coffee scones are a wonderful combination of rich coffee flavor and tender, buttery texture, making them a perfect addition to any breakfast or brunch spread. Enjoy!

Coffee Muffins

Ingredients:

- **For the Muffins:**
    - 1 1/2 cups (190 g) all-purpose flour
    - 1/2 cup (100 g) granulated sugar
    - 1/4 cup (50 g) packed brown sugar
    - 2 teaspoons baking powder
    - 1/2 teaspoon baking soda
    - 1/2 teaspoon salt
    - 1/2 cup (120 ml) strong brewed coffee (cooled)
    - 1/2 cup (120 ml) milk
    - 1/4 cup (60 ml) vegetable oil or melted butter
    - 1 large egg
    - 1 teaspoon vanilla extract
    - 1/2 cup (60 g) chopped nuts or chocolate chips (optional)
- **For the Streusel Topping (optional):**
    - 1/4 cup (30 g) all-purpose flour
    - 1/4 cup (50 g) granulated sugar
    - 1/4 cup (50 g) unsalted butter, cold and cut into small pieces
    - 1/2 teaspoon ground cinnamon

Instructions:

1. **Preheat Oven:**
    - Preheat your oven to 375°F (190°C). Line a muffin tin with paper liners or grease it lightly.
2. **Prepare Dry Ingredients:**
    - In a large bowl, whisk together the flour, granulated sugar, brown sugar, baking powder, baking soda, and salt.
3. **Combine Wet Ingredients:**
    - In a separate bowl, whisk together the cooled coffee, milk, vegetable oil (or melted butter), egg, and vanilla extract.
4. **Mix Wet and Dry Ingredients:**
    - Pour the wet ingredients into the dry ingredients. Stir until just combined. The batter will be slightly lumpy; do not overmix.
    - Fold in the chopped nuts or chocolate chips if using.
5. **Prepare Streusel Topping (optional):**
    - In a small bowl, mix together the flour, sugar, and ground cinnamon. Cut in the cold butter using a pastry cutter or your fingers until the mixture resembles coarse crumbs.
6. **Fill Muffin Tin:**
    - Divide the batter evenly among the muffin cups, filling each about 2/3 full.
    - If using, sprinkle the streusel topping evenly over the muffins.

7. **Bake:**
    - Bake in the preheated oven for 18-22 minutes, or until a toothpick inserted into the center of a muffin comes out clean.
8. **Cool:**
    - Allow the muffins to cool in the tin for 5 minutes before transferring them to a wire rack to cool completely.
9. **Serve:**
    - Enjoy the muffins warm or at room temperature, perfect with a cup of coffee or tea.

Tips:

- **Coffee Strength:** Use strong brewed coffee for a more pronounced coffee flavor. Adjust the amount to your taste preference.
- **Mix-ins:** Customize your muffins with other add-ins like dried fruit, seeds, or different types of chocolate.
- **Storage:** Store leftover muffins in an airtight container at room temperature for up to 3 days, or freeze for up to 2 months. To reheat, warm them in a microwave or oven.

These coffee muffins are a great way to enjoy your coffee in a new and delicious form. Enjoy the rich coffee flavor and tender texture of these tasty treats!

Coffee Shortbread Cookies

Ingredients:

- 1 cup (230 g) unsalted butter, softened
- 1/2 cup (100 g) granulated sugar
- 1/4 cup (50 g) packed brown sugar
- 2 tablespoons finely ground coffee or espresso powder
- 2 cups (240 g) all-purpose flour
- 1/4 teaspoon salt
- 1/2 teaspoon vanilla extract (optional)

Instructions:

1. **Preheat Oven:**
    - Preheat your oven to 350°F (175°C). Line a baking sheet with parchment paper or a silicone baking mat.
2. **Prepare the Dough:**
    - In a large bowl, cream together the softened butter, granulated sugar, and brown sugar until light and fluffy.
    - Add the finely ground coffee or espresso powder and mix until well incorporated.
    - Gradually add the flour and salt to the butter mixture. Mix until just combined. The dough will be crumbly but should hold together when pressed.
3. **Shape the Cookies:**
    - Turn the dough out onto a lightly floured surface. Gently knead the dough a few times to bring it together.
    - Roll out the dough to about 1/4-inch thickness. Use a cookie cutter to cut out shapes, or simply cut into squares or rectangles with a knife.
4. **Transfer to Baking Sheet:**
    - Place the cut-out cookies onto the prepared baking sheet, spacing them about 1 inch apart. If desired, you can use a fork to lightly press down on each cookie to create a decorative pattern.
5. **Bake:**
    - Bake in the preheated oven for 12-15 minutes, or until the edges are lightly golden. The centers will remain pale.
6. **Cool:**
    - Allow the cookies to cool on the baking sheet for 5 minutes before transferring them to a wire rack to cool completely.
7. **Serve:**
    - Enjoy the cookies on their own, or with a cup of coffee or tea.

Tips:

- **Coffee Flavor:** Adjust the amount of coffee or espresso powder to your taste preference. You can also use instant coffee for a smoother flavor.

- **Butter:** Make sure the butter is softened to room temperature for easy mixing.
- **Storage:** Store the cookies in an airtight container at room temperature for up to 1 week. They can also be frozen for up to 3 months. To freeze, layer the cookies between parchment paper and place in a freezer-safe container or bag.

These coffee shortbread cookies are a perfect blend of buttery richness and coffee flavor, making them a great choice for any coffee lover. Enjoy!

Coffee Chocolate Bark

Ingredients:

- 8 oz (225 g) semi-sweet or dark chocolate, chopped
- 1/4 cup (60 ml) strong brewed coffee or 1 tablespoon instant coffee granules
- 1/4 cup (30 g) finely chopped nuts (e.g., almonds, walnuts, or hazelnuts) or chocolate chips (optional)
- 1-2 tablespoons crushed coffee beans (optional, for added texture and flavor)
- Sea salt (optional, for sprinkling)

Instructions:

1. **Prepare Coffee:**
   - If using brewed coffee, ensure it's strong and cooled. If using instant coffee, dissolve the granules in a small amount of hot water to make a concentrated coffee.
2. **Melt the Chocolate:**
   - In a heatproof bowl, melt the chopped chocolate over a double boiler or in the microwave. If using the microwave, heat in 30-second intervals, stirring after each interval, until smooth and fully melted.
3. **Add Coffee:**
   - Once the chocolate is melted, stir in the brewed coffee or dissolved instant coffee. Mix until well combined and the coffee is fully incorporated into the chocolate.
4. **Prepare the Pan:**
   - Line a baking sheet or tray with parchment paper or a silicone baking mat.
5. **Spread the Chocolate:**
   - Pour the chocolate mixture onto the prepared baking sheet. Use a spatula to spread it into an even layer, about 1/4-inch thick.
6. **Add Toppings:**
   - Sprinkle the chopped nuts, chocolate chips, or crushed coffee beans evenly over the top of the chocolate.
   - If desired, sprinkle a pinch of sea salt over the top for a touch of contrast.
7. **Chill:**
   - Refrigerate the chocolate bark for about 30 minutes, or until it is completely set and hardened.
8. **Break into Pieces:**
   - Once set, break the chocolate bark into irregular pieces or squares.
9. **Serve and Store:**
   - Enjoy the coffee chocolate bark immediately, or store it in an airtight container at room temperature for up to 2 weeks. You can also refrigerate it to keep it firmer for a longer period.

Tips:

- **Chocolate Type:** Choose high-quality chocolate for the best flavor. You can also use milk chocolate or white chocolate if you prefer.
- **Coffee Strength:** Adjust the amount of coffee to your taste. A stronger coffee will impart a more pronounced flavor.
- **Toppings:** Feel free to customize with other toppings like dried fruit, crushed candies, or spices like cinnamon.

Coffee chocolate bark is a versatile and indulgent treat that combines the best of chocolate and coffee. It's easy to make and perfect for sharing or gifting. Enjoy!

Coffee Cupcakes

Ingredients:

- **For the Cupcakes:**
    - 1 1/2 cups (190 g) all-purpose flour
    - 1 cup (200 g) granulated sugar
    - 1/2 cup (115 g) unsalted butter, softened
    - 1/2 cup (120 ml) strong brewed coffee (cooled)
    - 1/4 cup (60 ml) milk
    - 2 large eggs
    - 1 teaspoon vanilla extract
    - 1 1/2 teaspoons baking powder
    - 1/4 teaspoon baking soda
    - 1/4 teaspoon salt
- **For the Coffee Frosting:**
    - 1/2 cup (115 g) unsalted butter, softened
    - 2 cups (240 g) powdered sugar
    - 2 tablespoons strong brewed coffee (cooled)
    - 1-2 tablespoons milk (if needed, to adjust consistency)
    - 1/2 teaspoon vanilla extract

Instructions:

1. **Preheat Oven:**
    - Preheat your oven to 350°F (175°C). Line a 12-cup muffin tin with paper liners.
2. **Prepare Dry Ingredients:**
    - In a medium bowl, whisk together the flour, baking powder, baking soda, and salt. Set aside.
3. **Cream Butter and Sugar:**
    - In a large bowl, cream together the softened butter and granulated sugar until light and fluffy.
4. **Add Eggs and Vanilla:**
    - Beat in the eggs, one at a time, until fully incorporated.
    - Mix in the vanilla extract.
5. **Combine Wet and Dry Ingredients:**
    - Gradually add the dry ingredients to the butter mixture, alternating with the brewed coffee and milk. Begin and end with the dry ingredients. Mix until just combined.
6. **Fill Muffin Tin:**
    - Divide the batter evenly among the 12 muffin cups, filling each about 2/3 full.
7. **Bake:**
    - Bake in the preheated oven for 18-22 minutes, or until a toothpick inserted into the center of a cupcake comes out clean.
8. **Cool:**

- Allow the cupcakes to cool in the tin for 5 minutes, then transfer them to a wire rack to cool completely.

9. **Prepare the Coffee Frosting:**
   - In a large bowl, beat the softened butter until creamy.
   - Gradually add the powdered sugar, beating until smooth.
   - Mix in the brewed coffee and vanilla extract. Beat until light and fluffy. If the frosting is too thick, add a little milk to reach your desired consistency.
10. **Frost the Cupcakes:**
    - Once the cupcakes are completely cooled, frost them with the coffee frosting using a piping bag or a spatula.
11. **Serve:**
    - Enjoy your coffee cupcakes with a cup of coffee or tea.

Tips:

- **Coffee Strength:** Use strong brewed coffee for a more pronounced flavor. You can adjust the amount to your taste.
- **Butter:** Ensure the butter is softened to room temperature for easy mixing and a smooth frosting.
- **Frosting Consistency:** Adjust the consistency of the frosting with additional milk if needed. It should be spreadable but not too runny.

Coffee cupcakes are a delicious and sophisticated treat, perfect for any coffee lover. They pair wonderfully with a cup of coffee or tea and make a lovely addition to any gathering. Enjoy!

Coffee Creme Fraiche Dip

Ingredients:

- 1 cup (240 ml) crème fraîche (or sour cream if crème fraîche is not available)
- 2 tablespoons strong brewed coffee (cooled) or 1 tablespoon instant coffee granules dissolved in 1 tablespoon hot water
- 2 tablespoons honey or maple syrup (adjust to taste)
- 1 teaspoon vanilla extract
- Pinch of salt
- Optional: 1-2 tablespoons finely chopped nuts or chocolate shavings for added texture

Instructions:

1. **Prepare Coffee:**
   - Brew a strong coffee and let it cool to room temperature. If using instant coffee, dissolve the granules in hot water and let it cool.
2. **Mix the Dip:**
   - In a medium bowl, combine the crème fraîche, cooled coffee, honey (or maple syrup), and vanilla extract. Stir until well mixed.
   - Add a pinch of salt to enhance the flavors and mix again.
3. **Adjust Sweetness:**
   - Taste the dip and adjust the sweetness if needed by adding more honey or maple syrup to your preference.
4. **Optional Add-ins:**
   - If using, fold in the finely chopped nuts or chocolate shavings for added texture and flavor.
5. **Chill:**
   - Refrigerate the dip for at least 30 minutes to allow the flavors to meld together and for it to thicken slightly.
6. **Serve:**
   - Serve the dip with fresh fruit (such as apple slices, berries, or pear slices), cookies, or as a spread for sweet bread or pastries.

Tips:

- **Crème Fraîche Substitute:** If you don't have crème fraîche, you can use sour cream or Greek yogurt as an alternative. Adjust the sweetness and coffee strength according to your taste.
- **Coffee Strength:** Adjust the amount of coffee based on how strong you want the coffee flavor to be.
- **Texture:** For a smoother texture, you can whisk the dip vigorously or use a hand mixer to combine the ingredients.

This coffee crème fraîche dip offers a creamy, tangy base with a rich coffee flavor, making it a versatile and tasty option for various pairings. Enjoy!

Coffee-Rubbed Steak

Ingredients:

- 2 (8-12 oz) steaks (e.g., ribeye, sirloin, or your preferred cut)
- 2 tablespoons finely ground coffee or espresso powder
- 1 tablespoon brown sugar
- 1 tablespoon paprika
- 1 teaspoon ground cumin
- 1 teaspoon garlic powder
- 1 teaspoon onion powder
- 1/2 teaspoon ground black pepper
- 1/2 teaspoon salt
- 1/2 teaspoon chili powder (optional, for extra heat)
- 1 tablespoon olive oil (for cooking)

Instructions:

1. **Prepare the Coffee Rub:**
   - In a small bowl, combine the finely ground coffee, brown sugar, paprika, ground cumin, garlic powder, onion powder, black pepper, salt, and chili powder (if using). Mix well.
2. **Season the Steaks:**
   - Pat the steaks dry with paper towels to ensure the rub adheres well.
   - Rub a generous amount of the coffee mixture onto both sides of each steak, pressing it in with your fingers. Let the steaks sit at room temperature for about 30 minutes to allow the flavors to penetrate.
3. **Preheat the Pan or Grill:**
   - If using a skillet, heat it over medium-high heat and add the olive oil. If using a grill, preheat it to high heat.
4. **Cook the Steaks:**
   - For a skillet: Once the oil is hot, add the steaks and cook to your desired doneness, about 4-6 minutes per side for medium-rare, depending on the thickness of the steaks. Use a meat thermometer to check the internal temperature (130°F / 54°C for medium-rare).
   - For a grill: Place the steaks on the grill and cook to your desired doneness, turning once halfway through the cooking time. Again, use a meat thermometer to ensure the correct internal temperature.
5. **Rest the Steaks:**
   - Remove the steaks from the heat and let them rest on a cutting board for 5-10 minutes before slicing. This allows the juices to redistribute throughout the meat.
6. **Serve:**
   - Slice the steaks against the grain and serve. They pair well with side dishes like roasted vegetables, mashed potatoes, or a simple green salad.

Tips:

- **Coffee Grind:** Use finely ground coffee or espresso powder for the rub to ensure a smooth texture and better flavor integration.
- **Cooking Method:** You can also cook the steaks in an oven if you prefer. Sear the steaks in a hot skillet to develop a crust, then transfer to a preheated oven at 375°F (190°C) to finish cooking.
- **Resting Time:** Letting the steak rest is crucial for a juicy result. Don't skip this step!

This coffee-rubbed steak is a flavorful and impressive dish that combines the deep richness of coffee with the savory goodness of steak. Enjoy your meal!

Coffee Chili

Ingredients:

- **For the Chili:**
    - 2 tablespoons olive oil
    - 1 large onion, finely chopped
    - 4 cloves garlic, minced
    - 1 bell pepper, diced (any color)
    - 1 pound (450 g) ground beef or ground turkey
    - 1/2 cup (120 ml) strong brewed coffee (cooled)
    - 1 (14.5 oz) can diced tomatoes
    - 1 (6 oz) can tomato paste
    - 1 (15 oz) can kidney beans, drained and rinsed
    - 1 (15 oz) can black beans, drained and rinsed
    - 1 tablespoon chili powder
    - 1 teaspoon ground cumin
    - 1 teaspoon paprika
    - 1/2 teaspoon ground oregano
    - 1/2 teaspoon cayenne pepper (optional, for extra heat)
    - Salt and black pepper to taste
- **For Garnish (optional):**
    - Shredded cheese
    - Chopped fresh cilantro
    - Sour cream
    - Sliced green onions
    - Sliced jalapeños

Instructions:

1. **Prepare Ingredients:**
    - Brew a strong coffee and let it cool. Prepare all vegetables and spices before starting.
2. **Cook the Vegetables:**
    - In a large pot or Dutch oven, heat the olive oil over medium heat.
    - Add the chopped onion and bell pepper. Cook until the onion is translucent and the bell pepper is softened, about 5-7 minutes.
    - Add the minced garlic and cook for an additional 1-2 minutes until fragrant.
3. **Cook the Meat:**
    - Add the ground beef or turkey to the pot. Cook until browned, breaking it up with a spoon as it cooks. Drain any excess fat if necessary.
4. **Add Coffee and Tomatoes:**
    - Pour in the brewed coffee, diced tomatoes, and tomato paste. Stir to combine.
5. **Add Beans and Spices:**

- Stir in the kidney beans, black beans, chili powder, cumin, paprika, oregano, and cayenne pepper (if using). Mix well.
6. **Simmer:**
    - Bring the chili to a boil, then reduce the heat to low. Cover and let it simmer for 30-45 minutes, stirring occasionally. This allows the flavors to meld together and the chili to thicken.
7. **Season to Taste:**
    - Taste the chili and adjust the seasoning with salt and black pepper as needed.
8. **Serve:**
    - Serve the chili hot, garnished with your choice of toppings like shredded cheese, chopped cilantro, sour cream, green onions, or jalapeños.

Tips:

- **Coffee Strength:** Use a strong coffee to get the best flavor. You can adjust the amount based on how prominent you want the coffee taste to be.
- **Beans:** Feel free to use other types of beans or adjust the quantities based on your preference.
- **Spice Level:** Adjust the cayenne pepper and chili powder to suit your taste and desired spice level.

Coffee chili is a hearty and flavorful dish that's perfect for a cozy dinner or a crowd-pleasing potluck. Enjoy the unique depth of flavor that the coffee brings to this classic comfort food!

Coffee-Infused Barbecue Sauce

Ingredients:

- 1 cup (240 ml) ketchup
- 1/2 cup (120 ml) strong brewed coffee (cooled)
- 1/4 cup (60 ml) apple cider vinegar
- 1/4 cup (60 g) brown sugar
- 2 tablespoons honey or maple syrup
- 2 tablespoons soy sauce
- 1 tablespoon Worcestershire sauce
- 1 tablespoon Dijon mustard
- 2 cloves garlic, minced
- 1 teaspoon smoked paprika
- 1/2 teaspoon ground cumin
- 1/2 teaspoon onion powder
- 1/4 teaspoon black pepper
- 1/4 teaspoon salt
- 1/4 teaspoon cayenne pepper (optional, for extra heat)

Instructions:

1. **Combine Ingredients:**
   - In a medium saucepan, combine the ketchup, brewed coffee, apple cider vinegar, brown sugar, honey (or maple syrup), soy sauce, Worcestershire sauce, Dijon mustard, and minced garlic. Stir well to combine.
2. **Add Spices:**
   - Stir in the smoked paprika, ground cumin, onion powder, black pepper, salt, and cayenne pepper (if using). Mix thoroughly.
3. **Simmer:**
   - Bring the mixture to a simmer over medium heat, stirring occasionally. Reduce the heat to low and continue to simmer for 15-20 minutes, or until the sauce has thickened and the flavors have melded together.
4. **Adjust Seasoning:**
   - Taste the sauce and adjust the seasoning if necessary. Add more salt, pepper, or sweetener to taste, if desired.
5. **Cool and Store:**
   - Allow the sauce to cool before using. Store it in an airtight container in the refrigerator for up to 2 weeks. The flavors will continue to develop and improve as it sits.
6. **Serve:**
   - Use the coffee-infused barbecue sauce as a glaze for grilled meats, a dipping sauce, or a condiment for sandwiches and burgers.

Tips:

- **Coffee Strength:** Use strong brewed coffee for a more pronounced coffee flavor. Adjust the amount to your taste preference.
- **Sweetness:** Adjust the sweetness with more or less brown sugar or honey according to your taste.
- **Consistency:** If the sauce is too thick, you can thin it out with a little more brewed coffee or water. If it's too thin, simmer it a bit longer to reduce and thicken.

This coffee-infused barbecue sauce adds a unique depth of flavor to your barbecue dishes, making it a standout condiment for your grilling adventures. Enjoy!

Coffee-Soaked Beef Brisket

Ingredients:

- **For the Brisket:**
    - 4-5 lbs (1.8-2.3 kg) beef brisket
    - 1 cup (240 ml) strong brewed coffee (cooled)
    - 1/2 cup (120 ml) beef broth or water
    - 1/4 cup (60 ml) soy sauce
    - 1/4 cup (60 ml) apple cider vinegar
    - 2 tablespoons brown sugar
    - 1 tablespoon Dijon mustard
    - 2 cloves garlic, minced
    - 1 tablespoon smoked paprika
    - 1 teaspoon ground cumin
    - 1 teaspoon onion powder
    - 1/2 teaspoon black pepper
    - 1/2 teaspoon salt
    - 1/2 teaspoon cayenne pepper (optional, for heat)
- **For the Rub (optional but recommended):**
    - 1 tablespoon ground coffee
    - 1 tablespoon paprika
    - 1 tablespoon brown sugar
    - 1 teaspoon garlic powder
    - 1 teaspoon onion powder
    - 1/2 teaspoon ground black pepper
    - 1/2 teaspoon salt

Instructions:

1. **Prepare the Brisket:**
    - Trim excess fat from the brisket, leaving a thin layer for flavor.
2. **Make the Marinade:**
    - In a bowl, combine the brewed coffee, beef broth (or water), soy sauce, apple cider vinegar, brown sugar, Dijon mustard, minced garlic, smoked paprika, ground cumin, onion powder, black pepper, salt, and cayenne pepper (if using). Stir until the sugar is dissolved and the mixture is well combined.
3. **Marinate the Brisket:**
    - Place the brisket in a large resealable plastic bag or a shallow dish. Pour the marinade over the brisket, making sure it's well coated. Seal the bag or cover the dish and refrigerate for at least 4 hours or overnight for best results.
4. **Prepare the Rub (optional):**
    - In a small bowl, mix together the ground coffee, paprika, brown sugar, garlic powder, onion powder, black pepper, and salt.
5. **Apply the Rub (optional):**

- Remove the brisket from the marinade and pat it dry with paper towels. Rub the brisket all over with the coffee rub mixture, pressing it in to adhere.

6. **Cook the Brisket:**
   - **Slow Cooker:** Place the brisket in a slow cooker. Pour a bit of the marinade over it (if desired). Cook on low for 8-10 hours, or until the brisket is tender and easily shreddable.
   - **Oven:** Preheat your oven to 300°F (150°C). Place the brisket in a roasting pan and cover with foil. Roast for 4-5 hours, or until the brisket is tender and easily shreds with a fork. You can also use a covered Dutch oven for this method.
   - **Grill (Indirect Heat):** Preheat the grill for indirect cooking. Place the brisket on the grill away from direct heat, cover, and cook for 4-5 hours, or until tender.
7. **Rest the Brisket:**
   - Remove the brisket from the heat and let it rest for 20 minutes before slicing. This helps the juices redistribute throughout the meat.
8. **Serve:**
   - Slice the brisket against the grain and serve with your favorite sides, such as roasted vegetables, mashed potatoes, or a fresh salad.

Tips:

- **Marinating Time:** For maximum flavor, marinate the brisket overnight.
- **Cooking Method:** Adjust cooking times based on the size of the brisket and your cooking method.
- **Resting Time:** Letting the brisket rest is essential for a juicy and flavorful result.

Coffee-soaked beef brisket is a rich, savory dish with a unique flavor profile that's sure to impress. Enjoy your meal!

Coffee-Glazed Chicken Wings

Ingredients:

- **For the Chicken Wings:**
    - 2 lbs (900 g) chicken wings
    - 1 tablespoon olive oil
    - Salt and black pepper to taste
- **For the Coffee Glaze:**
    - 1/2 cup (120 ml) strong brewed coffee (cooled)
    - 1/4 cup (60 ml) soy sauce
    - 1/4 cup (60 ml) honey or maple syrup
    - 2 tablespoons brown sugar
    - 1 tablespoon balsamic vinegar
    - 2 cloves garlic, minced
    - 1 teaspoon grated fresh ginger (or 1/2 teaspoon ground ginger)
    - 1/2 teaspoon crushed red pepper flakes (optional, for heat)
    - 1 tablespoon cornstarch mixed with 1 tablespoon water (for thickening, optional)

Instructions:

1. **Prepare the Wings:**
    - Preheat your oven to 425°F (220°C) or prepare your grill for indirect cooking.
    - Pat the chicken wings dry with paper towels. Toss them with olive oil, salt, and black pepper. Arrange the wings in a single layer on a baking sheet or grill pan.
2. **Bake or Grill the Wings:**
    - **Oven:** Bake in the preheated oven for 40-45 minutes, flipping halfway through, until the wings are crispy and golden brown.
    - **Grill:** Grill the wings over indirect heat, turning occasionally, for 25-30 minutes, or until they are cooked through and crispy.
3. **Prepare the Coffee Glaze:**
    - While the wings are cooking, make the glaze. In a small saucepan, combine the brewed coffee, soy sauce, honey (or maple syrup), brown sugar, balsamic vinegar, minced garlic, grated ginger, and crushed red pepper flakes (if using). Stir well to combine.
4. **Simmer the Glaze:**
    - Bring the mixture to a simmer over medium heat. Reduce the heat to low and let it simmer for 10-15 minutes, or until it has reduced slightly and thickened. If you want a thicker glaze, stir in the cornstarch mixture and continue to simmer for a few more minutes until it reaches your desired consistency.
5. **Glaze the Wings:**
    - Once the wings are cooked, transfer them to a large bowl. Pour the coffee glaze over the wings and toss until they are well coated.
6. **Serve:**

- Serve the glazed wings hot, garnished with fresh herbs like chopped parsley or cilantro if desired. They pair well with a side of celery sticks and a dipping sauce like ranch or blue cheese.

Tips:

- **Coffee Strength:** Use a strong brewed coffee for a more pronounced flavor. Adjust the amount of coffee and sweeteners based on your taste preference.
- **Glaze Thickness:** If the glaze is too thin, continue to simmer it to reduce further, or use the cornstarch mixture for thickening. If it's too thick, thin it out with a bit of water.
- **Cooking Method:** If you prefer, you can also pan-fry the wings for a crispier texture before glazing.

Coffee-glazed chicken wings offer a unique twist on a classic favorite, bringing rich, bold flavors to your next gathering or meal. Enjoy!

Coffee Marinade for Pork

Ingredients:

- 1/2 cup (120 ml) strong brewed coffee (cooled)
- 1/4 cup (60 ml) soy sauce
- 1/4 cup (60 ml) balsamic vinegar
- 2 tablespoons brown sugar
- 2 tablespoons olive oil
- 2 tablespoons Dijon mustard
- 2 cloves garlic, minced
- 1 tablespoon fresh rosemary, chopped (or 1 teaspoon dried rosemary)
- 1 teaspoon ground cumin
- 1/2 teaspoon smoked paprika
- 1/2 teaspoon black pepper
- 1/4 teaspoon salt

Instructions:

1. **Prepare the Marinade:**
   - In a bowl, whisk together the brewed coffee, soy sauce, balsamic vinegar, brown sugar, olive oil, Dijon mustard, minced garlic, chopped rosemary, ground cumin, smoked paprika, black pepper, and salt until well combined.
2. **Marinate the Pork:**
   - Place the pork (such as pork chops, pork tenderloin, or pork shoulder) in a resealable plastic bag or shallow dish.
   - Pour the marinade over the pork, making sure it is well-coated. Seal the bag or cover the dish with plastic wrap.
3. **Refrigerate:**
   - Refrigerate the pork and let it marinate for at least 2 hours, or overnight for best results. The longer it marinates, the more flavorful it will be.
4. **Cook the Pork:**
   - Remove the pork from the marinade and discard the excess marinade. Cook the pork according to your preferred method—grilling, roasting, or pan-searing—until it reaches the appropriate internal temperature (145°F / 63°C for pork chops and tenderloin).
5. **Serve:**
   - Allow the pork to rest for a few minutes before slicing and serving. This will help the juices redistribute and keep the meat moist.

Tips:

- **Coffee Strength:** Use strong brewed coffee for a more pronounced coffee flavor. Adjust the amount based on your taste preference.

- **Marinade Amount:** Adjust the marinade quantity based on the amount of pork you're using. You should have enough to cover the meat well.
- **Flavor Variations:** Feel free to experiment with other herbs and spices like thyme, paprika, or chili powder to customize the flavor to your liking.

This coffee marinade imparts a rich, deep flavor to pork, making it a standout dish at any meal. Enjoy the complex taste that the coffee brings to your pork!

Coffee-Flavored Whipped Cream

Ingredients:

- 1 cup (240 ml) heavy cream
- 2 tablespoons strong brewed coffee (cooled) or 1 tablespoon instant coffee granules dissolved in 1 tablespoon hot water
- 2 tablespoons powdered sugar
- 1 teaspoon vanilla extract

Instructions:

1. **Chill Your Equipment:**
   - For best results, chill your mixing bowl and beaters (or whisk) in the refrigerator for about 15-30 minutes before whipping. This helps the cream whip up better.
2. **Prepare the Coffee:**
   - Brew a strong coffee and let it cool. If using instant coffee, dissolve the granules in hot water and let it cool.
3. **Mix Ingredients:**
   - In the chilled mixing bowl, combine the heavy cream, cooled coffee (or coffee mixture), powdered sugar, and vanilla extract.
4. **Whip the Cream:**
   - Using an electric mixer or a hand whisk, beat the mixture on medium-high speed until soft peaks form. Be careful not to overwhip, as the cream can turn into butter if whipped too long.
5. **Adjust Sweetness and Coffee Flavor:**
   - Taste the whipped cream and adjust the sweetness or coffee flavor if needed. Add more powdered sugar or coffee to your liking and gently fold it in.
6. **Serve:**
   - Use the coffee-flavored whipped cream immediately or refrigerate it until ready to use. It's best used within a few hours but can be stored in the refrigerator for up to 24 hours.

Tips:

- **Coffee Strength:** Adjust the amount of coffee based on how strong you want the coffee flavor to be. For a more intense flavor, increase the coffee or use espresso.
- **Consistency:** If the whipped cream starts to separate or lose its structure, gently re-whip it before serving.
- **Flavor Variations:** You can also add a touch of cocoa powder or a splash of liqueur (like coffee liqueur) for additional flavor variations.

This coffee-flavored whipped cream adds a delightful twist to your desserts and coffee drinks, making them even more indulgent and enjoyable.

Coffee Syrup

Ingredients:

- 1 cup (240 ml) strong brewed coffee (cooled)
- 1 cup (200 g) granulated sugar
- 1/2 cup (100 g) brown sugar
- 1/4 cup (60 ml) water
- 1 tablespoon cornstarch
- 1/2 teaspoon vanilla extract
- 1/4 teaspoon salt

Instructions:

1. **Prepare the Coffee:**
    - Brew a strong cup of coffee and let it cool to room temperature.
2. **Combine Ingredients:**
    - In a medium saucepan, combine the brewed coffee, granulated sugar, brown sugar, and water. Stir well to dissolve the sugars.
3. **Cook the Syrup:**
    - Place the saucepan over medium heat and bring the mixture to a simmer, stirring occasionally.
    - In a small bowl, mix the cornstarch with a little cold water to create a slurry. Add this slurry to the simmering coffee mixture while stirring continuously.
4. **Simmer and Thicken:**
    - Continue to simmer the mixture for 10-15 minutes, or until it has thickened to a syrupy consistency. It should be thick enough to coat the back of a spoon.
5. **Add Vanilla and Salt:**
    - Stir in the vanilla extract and salt. Cook for an additional 1-2 minutes, then remove from heat.
6. **Cool and Store:**
    - Let the syrup cool to room temperature. Transfer it to a clean, airtight container or jar. Store in the refrigerator for up to 2-3 weeks.

Tips:

- **Coffee Strength:** Use strong brewed coffee to ensure the coffee flavor comes through in the syrup. Adjust the strength based on your taste preference.
- **Consistency:** The syrup will thicken further as it cools. If it becomes too thick, you can thin it out with a little more brewed coffee or water.
- **Flavor Variations:** Experiment with flavorings like a dash of cinnamon or a splash of coffee liqueur for a unique twist.

Uses:

- **Coffee Milk:** Mix a few tablespoons of coffee syrup with a glass of milk for a classic Rhode Island coffee milk.
- **Desserts:** Drizzle over ice cream, cakes, or pancakes for a rich coffee flavor.
- **Cocktails:** Use as a sweetener in coffee-based cocktails or as a flavor enhancer in mixed drinks.

This coffee syrup is a versatile and flavorful addition to many recipes, providing a deliciously sweet and robust coffee kick. Enjoy experimenting with it!

Coffee Pancakes

Ingredients:

- **For the Pancake Batter:**
    - 1 cup (120 g) all-purpose flour
    - 2 tablespoons granulated sugar
    - 1 tablespoon baking powder
    - 1/2 teaspoon salt
    - 1 large egg
    - 1 cup (240 ml) milk
    - 1/4 cup (60 ml) brewed coffee (cooled)
    - 2 tablespoons melted butter or vegetable oil
    - 1 teaspoon vanilla extract
- **For Serving (optional):**
    - Maple syrup
    - Whipped cream
    - Fresh berries or sliced bananas
    - Powdered sugar

Instructions:

1. **Prepare the Coffee:**
    - Brew a cup of strong coffee and let it cool to room temperature.
2. **Mix Dry Ingredients:**
    - In a large bowl, whisk together the flour, sugar, baking powder, and salt.
3. **Mix Wet Ingredients:**
    - In another bowl, whisk together the egg, milk, brewed coffee, melted butter (or oil), and vanilla extract until well combined.
4. **Combine Ingredients:**
    - Pour the wet ingredients into the dry ingredients. Stir gently until just combined. Be careful not to overmix; a few lumps are okay.
5. **Preheat the Pan:**
    - Heat a non-stick skillet or griddle over medium heat. Lightly grease with butter or oil if needed.
6. **Cook the Pancakes:**
    - Pour about 1/4 cup of batter onto the hot skillet for each pancake. Cook until bubbles form on the surface and the edges look set, about 2-3 minutes. Flip and cook until the other side is golden brown, about 1-2 more minutes.
7. **Serve:**
    - Keep the pancakes warm in a low oven while you cook the remaining pancakes. Serve warm with your favorite toppings like maple syrup, whipped cream, fresh berries, or a dusting of powdered sugar.

Tips:

- **Coffee Strength:** Use strong brewed coffee to ensure the coffee flavor comes through in the pancakes. You can adjust the amount of coffee to suit your taste.
- **Consistency:** If the batter is too thick, you can thin it out with a little more milk. If it's too thin, add a bit more flour.
- **Add-ins:** Feel free to mix in chocolate chips, nuts, or even a bit of cocoa powder for extra flavor.

Coffee pancakes are a wonderful way to enjoy the flavors of coffee in a comforting breakfast dish. They pair perfectly with a hot cup of coffee or a latte for a truly indulgent morning meal. Enjoy!

Coffee French Toast

Ingredients:

- **For the French Toast:**
    - 4 large eggs
    - 1 cup (240 ml) milk
    - 1/2 cup (120 ml) strong brewed coffee (cooled)
    - 2 tablespoons granulated sugar
    - 1 teaspoon vanilla extract
    - 1/2 teaspoon ground cinnamon
    - 1/4 teaspoon salt
    - 8 slices of bread (preferably thick, like challah, brioche, or Texas toast)
    - Butter or oil, for cooking
- **For Serving (optional):**
    - Maple syrup
    - Whipped cream
    - Fresh berries or sliced bananas
    - Powdered sugar

Instructions:

1. **Prepare the Coffee:**
    - Brew a cup of strong coffee and let it cool to room temperature.
2. **Make the Egg Mixture:**
    - In a large bowl, whisk together the eggs, milk, cooled coffee, granulated sugar, vanilla extract, ground cinnamon, and salt until well combined.
3. **Soak the Bread:**
    - Heat a large skillet or griddle over medium heat and add a little butter or oil to coat the surface.
    - Dip each slice of bread into the egg mixture, allowing it to soak for a few seconds on each side to absorb the liquid.
4. **Cook the French Toast:**
    - Place the soaked bread slices onto the hot skillet or griddle. Cook until golden brown on each side, about 2-3 minutes per side. Add more butter or oil to the pan as needed for cooking.
5. **Serve:**
    - Serve the coffee French toast warm, topped with your favorite toppings like maple syrup, whipped cream, fresh berries, or a dusting of powdered sugar.

Tips:

- **Bread Choice:** Use thick slices of bread like challah, brioche, or Texas toast for the best texture. Stale or day-old bread works well, as it soaks up the egg mixture better.

- **Coffee Strength:** Use strong brewed coffee to ensure the coffee flavor is prominent. Adjust the amount of coffee based on your taste preference.
- **Cooking:** Cook the French toast over medium heat to ensure it cooks through without burning.

Coffee French toast is a wonderful way to enjoy a coffee-flavored breakfast that's both comforting and indulgent. Enjoy your delicious coffee-infused French toast!

Coffee Smoothie

Ingredients:

- 1 cup (240 ml) brewed coffee (cooled) or 1/2 cup (120 ml) espresso
- 1 cup (240 ml) milk (any kind: dairy or non-dairy like almond, oat, or soy milk)
- 1 banana (preferably frozen for a creamier texture)
- 1/2 cup (120 ml) Greek yogurt or a non-dairy yogurt alternative
- 1 tablespoon honey or maple syrup (adjust to taste)
- 1/2 teaspoon vanilla extract
- 1/2 cup ice cubes (optional, for a colder and thicker smoothie)
- Optional add-ins: 1 tablespoon cocoa powder, a pinch of cinnamon, a handful of spinach, or a scoop of protein powder

Instructions:

1. **Prepare the Coffee:**
   - Brew a cup of coffee and let it cool to room temperature. If using espresso, let it cool as well.
2. **Blend Ingredients:**
   - In a blender, combine the cooled coffee, milk, banana, Greek yogurt, honey (or maple syrup), vanilla extract, and ice cubes (if using).
3. **Add Optional Ingredients:**
   - If you're adding cocoa powder, cinnamon, spinach, or protein powder, add them to the blender at this point.
4. **Blend Until Smooth:**
   - Blend on high speed until the mixture is smooth and creamy. If the smoothie is too thick, you can add a little more milk to reach your desired consistency.
5. **Serve:**
   - Pour the smoothie into a glass and enjoy immediately. You can also garnish with a sprinkle of cinnamon or a drizzle of chocolate syrup for extra flair.

Tips:

- **Frozen Banana:** Using a frozen banana will give your smoothie a thicker, creamier texture. If your banana is not frozen, you can add extra ice to achieve the same effect.
- **Coffee Strength:** Adjust the amount of coffee based on how strong you want the coffee flavor to be. If you prefer a stronger coffee taste, add more coffee or espresso.
- **Sweetness:** Adjust the sweetness with more or less honey or maple syrup according to your taste preference.
- **Flavor Variations:** Experiment with different flavorings like a scoop of vanilla or chocolate protein powder, a tablespoon of almond butter, or a dash of nutmeg.

This coffee smoothie is a refreshing and energizing way to enjoy your coffee and can be a great breakfast or snack option. Enjoy your smoothie!

Coffee Milkshake

Ingredients:

- 1 cup (240 ml) brewed coffee (cooled)
- 1/2 cup (120 ml) milk (any kind: dairy or non-dairy like almond, oat, or soy milk)
- 2 cups (300 g) vanilla ice cream
- 2 tablespoons granulated sugar (optional, adjust to taste)
- 1/2 teaspoon vanilla extract
- Whipped cream (optional, for topping)
- Chocolate syrup or caramel sauce (optional, for drizzling)

Instructions:

1. **Prepare the Coffee:**
   - Brew a cup of coffee and let it cool to room temperature. You can also use leftover coffee or cold brew coffee for convenience.
2. **Blend Ingredients:**
   - In a blender, combine the cooled coffee, milk, vanilla ice cream, and granulated sugar (if using). Add the vanilla extract.
3. **Blend Until Smooth:**
   - Blend on high speed until the mixture is smooth and creamy. If the milkshake is too thick, you can add a little more milk to reach your desired consistency.
4. **Serve:**
   - Pour the coffee milkshake into a glass. Top with whipped cream if desired, and drizzle with chocolate syrup or caramel sauce for extra indulgence.
5. **Garnish (optional):**
   - You can garnish with chocolate shavings, a sprinkle of cocoa powder, or a cherry on top.

Tips:

- **Coffee Strength:** Use strong brewed coffee for a more pronounced coffee flavor. Adjust the amount of coffee based on your taste preference.
- **Ice Cream Flavor:** Vanilla ice cream is traditional, but you can experiment with coffee-flavored or chocolate ice cream for different variations.
- **Sweetness:** Adjust the sweetness by adding more or less granulated sugar, or use flavored syrups like caramel or chocolate for additional sweetness and flavor.

This coffee milkshake is a delightful way to enjoy coffee in a creamy, refreshing form. It's perfect for a treat on a hot day or as a special dessert. Enjoy!

Coffee Infused Hot Chocolate

Ingredients:

- 2 cups (480 ml) milk (any kind: dairy or non-dairy like almond, oat, or soy milk)
- 1 cup (240 ml) brewed coffee (hot)
- 1/2 cup (100 g) semi-sweet chocolate chips or chopped chocolate
- 2 tablespoons cocoa powder
- 1/4 cup (50 g) granulated sugar (adjust to taste)
- 1/4 teaspoon salt
- 1/2 teaspoon vanilla extract

For Topping (optional):

- Whipped cream
- Chocolate shavings or cocoa powder
- Marshmallows

Instructions:

1. **Prepare the Coffee:**
   - Brew a cup of strong coffee and keep it hot.
2. **Heat the Milk:**
   - In a medium saucepan, heat the milk over medium heat until it's hot but not boiling.
3. **Combine Ingredients:**
   - Whisk in the cocoa powder, granulated sugar, and salt until well combined and smooth.
4. **Add Chocolate:**
   - Stir in the chocolate chips or chopped chocolate and continue to heat, whisking frequently, until the chocolate is completely melted and the mixture is smooth.
5. **Incorporate Coffee:**
   - Slowly add the hot brewed coffee to the chocolate mixture, stirring constantly until well blended.
6. **Add Vanilla:**
   - Remove the saucepan from heat and stir in the vanilla extract.
7. **Serve:**
   - Pour the coffee-infused hot chocolate into mugs. Top with whipped cream, chocolate shavings, or marshmallows if desired.

Tips:

- **Chocolate Type:** Use high-quality chocolate for the best flavor. Semi-sweet chocolate works well, but you can also use milk chocolate or dark chocolate based on your preference.

- **Coffee Strength:** Adjust the amount of coffee to your taste. For a stronger coffee flavor, use more coffee or a stronger brew.
- **Sweetness:** Taste the hot chocolate and adjust the sweetness if needed by adding more sugar or sweetened whipped cream.
- **Serving Ideas:** For a festive touch, sprinkle a little cinnamon or nutmeg on top of the whipped cream.

This coffee-infused hot chocolate is a comforting and indulgent drink that combines the best of both coffee and chocolate worlds. Enjoy this cozy treat!

Coffee Poached Pears

Ingredients:

- 4 ripe but firm pears (e.g., Bosc or Anjou)
- 2 cups (480 ml) brewed coffee (cooled)
- 1 cup (240 ml) water
- 1 cup (200 g) granulated sugar
- 1/2 cup (120 ml) red or white wine (optional, for added depth of flavor)
- 1/4 cup (60 ml) honey
- 1 cinnamon stick
- 2-3 whole cloves
- 1 vanilla bean (split and scraped) or 1 teaspoon vanilla extract
- 1 tablespoon lemon juice
- Optional garnish: whipped cream, chocolate shavings, or nuts

Instructions:

1. **Prepare the Pears:**
   - Peel the pears, leaving the stems intact. Cut a small slice off the bottom of each pear so they sit upright.
2. **Prepare the Poaching Liquid:**
   - In a large saucepan, combine the brewed coffee, water, granulated sugar, red or white wine (if using), honey, cinnamon stick, cloves, and vanilla bean (or vanilla extract). Stir until the sugar is dissolved.
3. **Add Lemon Juice:**
   - Stir in the lemon juice.
4. **Poach the Pears:**
   - Carefully add the pears to the saucepan. The pears should be mostly submerged in the liquid. If needed, add a bit more water or coffee to cover the pears.
   - Bring the liquid to a simmer over medium heat. Reduce the heat to low and gently simmer the pears for 20-30 minutes, or until they are tender when pierced with a fork. The exact time will depend on the size and ripeness of the pears.
5. **Reduce the Liquid (Optional):**
   - If you prefer a thicker syrup, remove the pears from the saucepan once they are done. Increase the heat and simmer the poaching liquid for an additional 10-15 minutes, or until it has reduced to a thicker consistency.
6. **Cool the Pears:**
   - Allow the pears to cool in the poaching liquid. They can be served warm or chilled. If serving chilled, transfer the pears to the refrigerator to chill for a few hours or overnight.
7. **Serve:**
   - Arrange the pears on serving plates. Spoon some of the reduced poaching liquid over the pears. Garnish with whipped cream, chocolate shavings, or nuts if desired.

Tips:

- **Pears:** Choose pears that are ripe but still firm, as they will hold their shape better during poaching.
- **Coffee Strength:** Use a strong brewed coffee for a more pronounced coffee flavor. Adjust the amount based on your taste preference.
- **Wine:** The wine adds complexity to the poaching liquid, but you can omit it if you prefer or use a non-alcoholic substitute.

Coffee-poached pears are a sophisticated and delicious dessert that pairs beautifully with the coffee flavor. Enjoy this elegant treat!

Coffee and Nut Clusters

Ingredients:

- 1 cup (240 ml) brewed coffee (strong and cooled)
- 2 cups (200 g) mixed nuts (such as almonds, cashews, walnuts, or pecans), roughly chopped
- 1 cup (175 g) semisweet or dark chocolate chips
- 1/4 cup (50 g) granulated sugar
- 1 tablespoon instant coffee granules (optional, for extra coffee flavor)
- 1/2 teaspoon vanilla extract
- Pinch of salt

Instructions:

1. **Prepare the Coffee:**
   - Brew a strong cup of coffee and let it cool to room temperature. If using instant coffee granules for an extra boost, dissolve them in the brewed coffee.
2. **Toast the Nuts:**
   - Preheat your oven to 350°F (175°C). Spread the nuts in a single layer on a baking sheet and toast for about 5-7 minutes, or until fragrant and slightly golden. Stir occasionally to ensure even toasting. Let the nuts cool.
3. **Melt the Chocolate:**
   - In a heatproof bowl, melt the chocolate chips over a double boiler or in the microwave in 30-second intervals, stirring between each interval until smooth.
4. **Combine Ingredients:**
   - In a large bowl, mix the toasted nuts with the melted chocolate. Stir until the nuts are well coated.
5. **Add Coffee Flavor:**
   - Stir in the cooled brewed coffee, granulated sugar, instant coffee granules (if using), vanilla extract, and a pinch of salt. Mix until everything is evenly combined.
6. **Form the Clusters:**
   - Drop spoonfuls of the nut and chocolate mixture onto a baking sheet lined with parchment paper. You can shape them into clusters or mounds, depending on your preference.
7. **Chill:**
   - Refrigerate the clusters for at least 30 minutes, or until the chocolate is set and firm.
8. **Serve:**
   - Once the chocolate has set, the clusters are ready to enjoy. Store them in an airtight container at room temperature for up to a week or in the refrigerator for longer shelf life.

Tips:

- **Nuts:** Use your favorite combination of nuts or a single type if you prefer. Ensure they are chopped into bite-sized pieces for easy snacking.
- **Coffee Strength:** Adjust the strength of the coffee based on your preference. Stronger coffee will give a more pronounced coffee flavor.
- **Sweetness:** If you prefer a sweeter treat, you can add a bit more sugar or even some sweetened condensed milk to the chocolate mixture.

These coffee and nut clusters are a perfect blend of coffee and crunchy nuts, making them a great snack or gift option. Enjoy!

Coffee Custard

Ingredients:

- 2 cups (480 ml) milk (any kind: dairy or non-dairy like almond, oat, or soy milk)
- 1 cup (240 ml) brewed coffee (cooled, strong)
- 4 large egg yolks
- 1/2 cup (100 g) granulated sugar
- 1/4 cup (60 ml) heavy cream
- 1 teaspoon vanilla extract
- 1/4 teaspoon salt

Instructions:

1. **Prepare the Oven and Ramekins:**
   - Preheat your oven to 325°F (160°C). Place 4-6 ramekins (or custard cups) in a baking dish. You will be using the baking dish to create a water bath for the custards.
2. **Heat the Milk and Coffee:**
   - In a medium saucepan, combine the milk and brewed coffee. Heat over medium heat until it's hot but not boiling, stirring occasionally. Remove from heat.
3. **Mix Egg Yolks and Sugar:**
   - In a bowl, whisk together the egg yolks and granulated sugar until the mixture is light and slightly thickened.
4. **Temper the Egg Mixture:**
   - Slowly pour a small amount of the hot milk and coffee mixture into the egg yolks, whisking constantly to temper the eggs and prevent them from curdling.
5. **Combine Mixtures:**
   - Gradually whisk the tempered egg yolks back into the remaining milk and coffee mixture in the saucepan. Stir well to combine.
6. **Add Vanilla and Salt:**
   - Stir in the vanilla extract and salt.
7. **Strain the Mixture (Optional):**
   - For a smoother texture, strain the custard mixture through a fine-mesh sieve into a large measuring cup or bowl to remove any curdled bits.
8. **Pour into Ramekins:**
   - Divide the custard mixture evenly among the prepared ramekins.
9. **Prepare the Water Bath:**
   - Fill the baking dish with hot water until it reaches halfway up the sides of the ramekins. This helps to cook the custards gently and evenly.
10. **Bake the Custards:**
    - Bake in the preheated oven for 30-40 minutes, or until the custards are set but still slightly jiggly in the center. A knife inserted into the center should come out clean or with just a few moist crumbs.
11. **Cool and Serve:**

- Remove the ramekins from the water bath and let them cool to room temperature. Refrigerate for at least 2 hours or until well chilled.
12. **Garnish (Optional):**
    - Before serving, you can garnish with a dollop of whipped cream, a sprinkle of cocoa powder, or a few coffee beans for decoration.

Tips:

- **Coffee Strength:** Use a strong coffee for a more pronounced coffee flavor in the custard. Adjust the amount of coffee based on your taste preference.
- **Custard Consistency:** Be careful not to overcook the custard. It should be set but still creamy. The residual heat will continue to cook the custard slightly after you remove it from the oven.
- **Straining:** Straining the custard mixture helps ensure a smooth and silky texture.

This coffee custard is a rich and comforting dessert with a wonderful coffee flavor. It's perfect for special occasions or a delicious treat to enjoy anytime.

www.ingramcontent.com/pod-product-compliance
Lightning Source LLC
LaVergne TN
LVHW081609060526
838201LV00054B/2165